The
Daily Book
of
Positive Quotations

The
Daily Book
of
Positive
Quotations

LINDA PICONE

Fairview Press

Minneapolis

Published by Fairview Press, 2450 Riverside Avenue, Minneapolis,
MN 55454. For a free catalog of Fairview Press titles, call toll-free
1-800-544-8207, or visit our website at www.fairviewpress.org.

Fairview Press is a division of Fairview Health Services, a community-
focused health system, affiliated with the University of Minnesota,
providing a complete range of services, from the prevention of illness
and injury to care for the most complex medical conditions.

Library of Congress Cataloging-in-Publication Data
The daily book of positive quotations / Linda Picone.
    p. cm.
  ISBN-13: 978-1-57749-174-3 (alk. paper)
  1. Quotations, English. 2. Motivation (Psychology)--Quotations,
maxims, etc. 3. Inspiration--Quotations, maxims, etc. I. Picone,
Linda.
  PN6081.D14 2008

                                              081--dc22

Typography: Dorie McClelland, Spring Book Design
Printed in Canada
First printing: January 2008

Introduction

Collected on these pages are quotations from some of the world's greatest thinkers on living life well. Some are funny. Some are spiritual. Some are encouraging. Some are provocative.

And some contradict each other: Have many friends—or only a few. Work with intention towards your goals—or let life take you by surprise. Tread cautiously—or cherish your mistakes. Listen to others—or rely on your own judgment.

The point of this book is not to give you a fixed itinerary as you make your way on the road of life but rather to offer some bright stars you might use to set your own course.

Following each quotation is a sentence or two to help you think about the idea expressed in the quotation. This daily reading may include a question for you to answer, a statement for you to accept or reject, or a pledge for you to make.

Each new day, you are invited to read a quotation and consider the discussion. Do you agree? Disagree? Is this a new idea for you, or does it confirm something you already believe? Is the message a call to action, or an opportunity for contemplation?

You may have a very different understanding of a particular quotation than what is suggested here. Feel free to let your thoughts take you where they will. In fact, you may find that rereading the quotation at another time, or reading a similar quotation, causes your thoughts to go in yet another direction. For this reason, you may want to read and reread entries regardless of what day it is. (There is no entry for February 29, so at least every four years you will have a good reason to reread a favorite affirmation.)

However you choose to use the book, the hope is that the wisdom you find here will help you face each new day with greater strength and a more positive outlook.

The
Daily Book
of
Positive Quotations

Little things

> *"One resolution I have made, and try always to keep, is this: To rise above the little things."*
>
> ❧JOHN BURROUGHS☙

The faucet is leaking, we walk out of the house with mismatched socks, we run out of milk, we're low on gas, the yard needs mowing, we forget to thaw some meat for dinner—these sorts of trivial issues can pile up to ruin a day. But only if we let them.

We can't think big thoughts all the time, but we can keep the little things in perspective and not let their sheer numbers overwhelm us.

I'm going to take a deep breath—maybe even two or three deep breaths—and remind myself that as annoying as the minor problems of everyday life are, I'm not going to fret about them.

Things change

> "*Sometimes our fate resembles a fruit tree in winter. Who would think that those branches would turn green again and blossom, but we hope it, we know it.*"
> ❧JOHANN WOLFGANG VON GOETHE❧

When our lives are difficult, we feel as if things will never change. This, in turn, makes it harder for us to take the steps that might create the change we want.

When we look back on our lives, we can see that we've had both good and bad times. Somehow, we survived the bad times, and things eventually got better. The passage of time helped, but we also acted in ways that moved us towards a happier place.

My life is filled with ups and downs. If today is a bad day—or this week is a bad week—I know it's not forever and that I will come through it.

Self-talk

"People don't just get upset. They contribute to their upsetness."

❧ALBERT ELLIS❧

It's not the events in our lives that upset us. It's how we think about them. If something bad happens, we may complain and fear we'll never feel better again.

But someone else in the same situation might say, "Gee, that's too bad, but I know I can handle it." The same event, two different perspectives. We can't control many of the things that happen to us, but we can control how we react to them.

I'd like things to go my way, but, really, there's nothing that says they should. I need to remind myself that I have what it takes to improve my mood—and my life.

Keeping perspective

"When I hear somebody sigh that life is hard, I am always tempted to ask, 'Compared to what?'"
SYDNEY J. HARRIS

We like to compare our lives to those of people we think are richer, smarter, happier, better looking, more famous. Why don't we have a house like the couple's down the street? Why aren't we doing better at work? Why can't we find the love of our life?

We forget that there are plenty of people who look on *us* with envy. They would really like to have our job, live on our block, or enjoy our personal freedom. When we hear them talk about the things we take for granted, we remember that we have it pretty good after all.

It might sound corny, but it does help to "count my blessings" so I can pay attention to all the good things in my life.

Making others happy

"Happiness is a perfume you cannot pour on others without getting a few drops on yourself."
RALPH WALDO EMERSON

There is a reason we do volunteer work, bring flowers to a friend in the hospital, or buy a special gift for someone we love when we're out shopping: It makes us happy. Sometimes, in fact, being kind and considerate to others actually benefits us more than the people we're helping.

Even if our activity starts out as a chore or an obligation, rather than something from the heart, it can become a joy to us, as well as to those who benefit from our efforts.

Is there something I can do to delight another person today? It doesn't have to be big or spectacular. A simple message expressing how much I appreciate someone's friendship can be very powerful.

Just one thing

"Nothing is particularly hard if you divide it into small jobs."

◆HENRY FORD◆

The pile of papers on the desk keeps getting bigger. The dishes in the sink seem to be multiplying on their own. We've got too much to do at work and at home, and it all seems overwhelming. We toss and turn through the night, wondering how we'll ever get it all done.

But if every time we walk into a room we take care of just one piece of paper or wash just one dish, gradually that pile of papers will get smaller, and the dishes will be cleaned, and we'll be able to sleep again.

Instead of panicking over how much I have to do, I'm going to pick one thing and do it. When it's done, I'll pick something else and do that.

Vision

> ❝*You got to be careful if you don't know where you're going, because you might not get there.*❞
> ❧YOGI BERRA❧

Do we have a clear vision of where we want our lives to go? Or do we just react to things as they happen? Sometimes we need to do a little of both. Without an idea of what we hope to be and accomplish, we may not achieve our full potential.

On the other hand, when exciting opportunities present themselves, sometimes the best thing to do is go with them, whether or not they fit perfectly into the plan we've made for ourselves.

I can spend a little time today thinking about how my daily activities fit with my goals. Am I spending too much time on distractions and not enough time on the things that will help me get where I want to go? Am I open to new opportunities when they present themselves?

Difficult times

"I ask not for a lighter burden but for broader shoulders."

⟋JEWISH PROVERB⟍

Learning to handle problems is like lifting weights: The more we do, the stronger we become.

None of us wish for problems, of course, but when they come along—and we all must face problems in our lives—we can take solace in knowing that we are gaining coping skills that will help us in the future.

I have learned a lot from the most difficult times in my life, and I am a stronger person as a result.

Smiling

66*Sometimes your joy is the source of your smile,
but sometimes your smile can be the source of
your joy.*99

❧THICH NHAT HANH☙

Physiologically, it's been shown that smiling can
make us feel happy, even if we are forcing the
smile deliberately.

Regardless of the science, it makes sense to
smile, whether we feel like it or not. A smile
energizes our brain as well as our muscles. And
we don't want our face to settle into sadness.

As silly as it may seem, I'm going to remind myself
to smile regularly today, and then I'll see what
happens.

Day by day

> "*How we spend our days is, of course, how we spend our lives.*"
>
> ~ANNIE DILLARD~

Next week, next month, next summer . . . *that's* when the good times will come. But right now we're just trying to get through today, and maybe tomorrow, and, with luck, the day after that.

Let's not miss our lives while they're happening. We can make choices about what we want to do right this moment. Sure, the garbage still needs to be taken out and work has to be done, but even in the rush of the everyday we can take time to appreciate what we have.

I'll give myself a few minutes to appreciate a beautiful sunrise, the comfort of my warm bed, the sheer joy of a baby's laugh, or even the pleasure of solitude—whatever my life holds today.

Making opportunities

> "*Opportunity is missed by most people because it is dressed in overalls and looks like work.*"
> ❧THOMAS EDISON❧

Other people get all the breaks, don't they? Or so we tell ourselves. While it's true that sometimes others really do get a break, we could do a lot more to create our own breaks if we really wanted to.

Did we skip an opportunity to get some training because it was scheduled after work hours? Did we pass up a chance to try something new because we were nervous about whether we could do it? Maybe it's time to roll up our sleeves and work a little harder or longer.

How can I create my own opportunity—at work or in my personal life? What steps do I need to take?

Laughing at ourselves

*"Angels can fly because they take themselves
lightly; devils fall because of their gravity."*
G.K. CHESTERTON

We are at the center of the drama that is our life
and, like actors hamming it up, we sometimes
play our role with excessive amounts of
emotion, self-importance, and shouting.

We'd be a lot more effective—and a lot more
fun to be around—if we thought of our lives as
a comedy. A comedy with a moral, perhaps, and
filled with gentle laughter rather than howls—a
comedy that recognizes that there's more to the
world than what we do or think.

I recognize that the things I do—my accomplish-
ments and my mistakes—are not insignificant,
but if I take things too seriously, life won't be fun.
Humor can help me keep things in perspective.

A balance in life

"There are as many nights as days, and the one is just as long as the other in the year's course. Even a happy life cannot be without a measure of darkness, and the word happy *would lose its meaning if it were not balanced by sadness."*

◆ CARL GUSTAV JUNG ◆

Wouldn't it be wonderful if we never had a problem or a bad day?

And yet the sunshine after a storm is often brighter and more pleasurable than the sunshine after a string of cloudless days. Happiness that follows a troubled time can be more intense—or at least more appreciated—than happiness in the midst of an easy time.

If I feel like things are not going well right now, I'll think about how good it's going to feel when I get through this—and I *will* get through this.

Stages

"*Start by doing what's necessary, then what's possible, and suddenly you are doing the impossible.*"

ST. FRANCIS OF ASSISI

One step at a time, one step at a time—that's all we can do. But it can be more than enough. There are things we have to do each day: go to work, care for a child, prepare a meal. And there are things we do because we want to: volunteer for a community organization, host a party for a friend, plant a garden.

We bustle about happily doing all that we need to do, plus the things that bring pleasure to ourselves and others. We might be intimidated by the amount of work involved, but by simply doing things we can accomplish more than we think.

Instead of thinking about how I can't possibly do something I want to do, I'll just start doing what I can and see where it leads.

Making changes

*"They say that time changes things, but you
actually have to change them yourself."*
❧ ANDY WARHOL ❧

We often think of time as a powerful healer.
Sometimes we wish we could just go to sleep
and wake up six months or a year later, so we
wouldn't have to suffer through what we're
suffering now.

But time doesn't change things. It's the
work we do while time is passing that changes
things. The good news is, we don't have to wait
six months or a year or even a minute to start
this work.

If I know I'll feel better about something six
months from now, what can I do today that will
help me feel at least a little better now?

Creative thinking

> " *The best way to have a good idea is to have lots of ideas.* "
>
> ❧ LINUS PAULING ☙

We are much more creative than we give ourselves credit for. The problem is that we often suppress our ideas too quickly: No, that won't work. Can't afford that. Wouldn't enjoy that.

If we can have the courage not to censor our ideas, we might surprise and delight ourselves.

I will free my mind today and see how many interesting ideas I can come up with. Even if it turns out that none of them have practical value, I will still benefit from the creativity that I set free.

Sleep's value

"Early to bed and early to rise,
Makes a man healthy, wealthy, and wise."
~ BENJAMIN FRANKLIN ~

It's lovely to sink into a warm bed, close our eyes, and let the world fall away. A good night's sleep helps our bodies and minds recover from the stress of the day.

When we go to bed early, we can wake up early. And when we wake up early, we have a jump-start on the day. We can use the time to write in a journal, take a quiet walk, or meditate—things hard to squeeze in once the day gets busy.

I'll make a "date" with myself to go to sleep early tonight, snuggling into my own cozy bed and enjoying the luxury of slumber.

Giving our all

"Throw your heart over the fence and the rest will follow."
NORMAN VINCENT PEALE

To keep from being disappointed, we sometimes lower our expectations or avoid taking chances. There can be good reasons for this, but it can limit what we experience.

When we follow our heart, even at the risk of disappointment and pain, a world opens up we might not otherwise have entered: a job that takes us in new and exciting directions; friends we wouldn't have guessed would "fit" in our lives; experiences we didn't expect.

I will keep my expectations high and look for what excites me. I will risk disappointment to follow my heart.

Laughing everyday

"*Laughter is the sun that drives winter from the human face.*"

❧ VICTOR HUGO ☙

Even a baby responds happily to the sound of laughter. "I can't just make myself laugh," we say when someone chides us for being grumpy. But we can. Every day is full of amusing moments— if we take time to notice and appreciate them. We can even laugh at ourselves.

I will laugh wholeheartedly today.

Keeping friends

"People, even more than things, have to be restored, renewed, revived, reclaimed, and redeemed; never throw out anyone."
> ～AUDREY HEPBURN～

As we go through life, we make—and lose—many friendships. "We grew apart," we say when a friendship we valued drops away. We stop seeing friends who were once close to us because our lives have gone different directions.

But it can take only a little effort to keep "lost" friends in our lives. Perhaps the friendship has changed. The person we used to talk to every day is now someone we see only once or twice a year. But our life is richer for keeping this person in it.

What friend have I not talked to in far too long? I will reach out today, by phone, letter, or email.

Letting go

"Pick battles big enough to matter, small enough to win."

~ JONATHAN KOZOL ~

The flip side of "don't sweat the small stuff" is fighting for the things we care about. At the same time, we should try to avoid battles we have absolutely no chance of winning.

In general, things that help us be the person we most want to be are the things worth fighting for. Those that don't have much impact—or that may even detract from our best self—need to be let go.

Of the possible battles I may face today, which really matter? And of those that matter, which will make the biggest difference if I fight them?

The miracle of life

> *"The miracle is not to fly in the air, or to walk on the water, but to walk on the earth."*
>
> **CHINESE PROVERB**

To be born, to grow, to walk among the wonders of nature, to live a life of dignity, humor, and grace—this is the miracle of existence.

The complexity and possibility of our lives can fill us with awe. We should never take the miracle of life for granted.

Today I will remember how extraordinary even my ordinary life is.

Laughing in adversity

"*Life does not cease to be funny when people die any more than it ceases to be serious when people laugh.*"
～GEORGE BERNARD SHAW～

How can we laugh and have fun when so many bad things are going on around us? Isn't it wrong to enjoy ourselves when others are going through difficult times?

Laughter is a gift that can help us through difficult times. We shouldn't be ashamed of smiling when life seems bleak.

Laughing may not solve my problems today, but it may very well help me cope with them.

Simpler times

"*Firelight will not let you read fine stories, but it's
warm and you won't see the dust on the floor.*"
IRISH PROVERB

The most luxurious homes are no more comfortable in a snowstorm than a warm, dry cabin in the woods. The niceties of life mean little when our needs are simple: warmth when we're cold; food when we're hungry; sleep when we're tired.

We wish for so many things that we think will bring us happiness. Yet we often find ourselves looking back fondly on simpler times.

What small things in my life bring me pleasure?
I will recognize them today, and be thankful for
them.

Kindness

" Three things in human life are important.
The first is to be kind.
The second is to be kind.
The third is to be kind. "

❧ HENRY JAMES ☙

Doctors pledge to "first, do no harm." We can go one step further: First, we will be kind. Let us approach every situation looking for ways to be kind to others. Even if our kindness isn't returned, we will be better for setting an example and living up to our principles.

Today I will do at least one kind thing for someone else.

Thankfulness

"*Let us rise up and be thankful,*
for if we didn't learn a lot today,
at least we learned a little,
and if we didn't learn a little,
at least we didn't get sick,
and if we got sick, at least we didn't die;
so, let us all be thankful."

🙟 BUDDHA 🙝

Doesn't it seem as if the people with the most problems are often those who are most thankful for what they have? Facing a crisis tends to make us appreciate the things we take for granted.

Our challenge is to appreciate what we have, even without a crisis to prompt us.

I will start and end today thinking about how fortunate I am, right here, right now.

Spreading joy

"The best way to cheer yourself up is to try to cheer somebody else up."

🪶MARK TWAIN🪶

When we help others cope with their problems, it somehow makes our own seem less pressing. The advice we give—count your blessings; this, too, will pass; what doesn't kill us makes us stronger—can't help but affect our own thinking.

If we distract others from whatever it is that's weighing on them, we'll be distracted from our own burdens as well.

Do I know someone who's struggling? What can I do to help?

Giving

"In charity there is no excess."
SIR FRANCIS BACON

As the saying goes, "Give until it hurts." But true, selfless giving—of ourselves as well as our possessions—should never hurt. The more we freely and willingly give to others, the more we give to ourselves.

I will offer myself in some way that is helpful to others, without resenting the time or effort it takes.

Courage

> *"Courage is doing what you're afraid to do.*
> *There can be no courage unless you're scared."*
> ❧EDDIE RICKENBACKER❧

Some of us seem to never fear failure. But do we just hide our fear really well? Others of us acknowledge our fear, even when doing so may feel embarrassing. We may be afraid of falling flat on our faces, but we stand up straight and do our best.

It's okay for me to be afraid. I can admit this to myself and others and still tackle the things that frighten me.

Good deeds

> "*Humankind's ladder to God is a ladder of deeds.*"
>
> ❧ SHOLEM ASCH ❧

Talk about the importance of faith and morality is, in the end, just talk. It's what we do that matters.

Virtually every religion has some version of the Golden Rule: Behave towards others as you'd like them to behave towards you. Given this fact, it's surprising how seldom we see the Golden Rule in action.

What one thing can I do today that will directly reflect my beliefs?

Strength in adversity

"Adversity draws men together and produces beauty and harmony in life's relationships, just as the cold of winter produces ice-flowers on the windowpanes, which vanish with the warmth."
SØREN KIERKEGAARD

We see it after every major disaster: People opening their hearts, their homes, and their wallets to help others. On a smaller, more personal scale, friends help each other in times of adversity—and even strangers rise to acts of heroism when the situation demands it.

We all have within us the desire and ability to help others. It's too bad that we forget this until adversity strikes.

If I would help someone in a disaster, why can't I help someone right now, when there is no disaster? What small thing can I do today for someone, even someone I don't know?

Thinking and spirituality

"Zen does not confuse spirituality with thinking about God while one is peeling potatoes. Zen spirituality is just to peel the potatoes."
ALAN W. WATTS

We rarely allow ourselves to be in the world without *thinking* about it. Seldom do we look at a beautiful sunset without turning to someone to say, "Isn't that a beautiful sunset?" Worse, our thinking can distract or occupy us so much that we don't even notice the sunset in the first place.

There is value in being mindful of the world and what it offers without comment or thought. To be present in the moment—feeling the warmth of the sun on our skin; breathing in the cool, crisp air; listening to the chirp-chirp of birds in the early morning.

I will close my eyes and allow myself to be in the world—and the world to be in me—without trying to attach words to what I am experiencing.

Living every day

"May you live all the days of your life."
JONATHAN SWIFT

How often do we ask ourselves, as if waking from a dream, "Where has the time gone? What happened to yesterday? last week? last month? last year?"

Our lives are all that we have on earth, and yet how many days do we let slip by without living them as fully as we might?

Living every day doesn't have to mean trying to achieve something significant every moment that we're conscious. No one could sustain a life like that. It just means doing something each day that adds value to our lives and the lives of others.

I will do something today that will make me feel that I have really lived it.

Taking chances

" Chance is always powerful. Let your hook be always cast; in the pool, where you least expect it, there will be a fish. "

❧ OVID ❧

We can't get into a college or find a new job if we don't try. Those that we think of as being lucky are often simply those who have been willing to take a chance, to put themselves on the line.

We often talk ourselves out of exploring opportunities, because we're convinced that there is little chance we would succeed. But if we aren't willing to put our hook in the pool, it's guaranteed that we will never catch a fish.

I will look for an opportunity I might otherwise pass by and take a chance on it.

Character

"People seem not to see that their opinion of the
world is also a confession of their character."
RALPH WALDO EMERSON

The world isn't especially concerned with
making us happy, as much as we would like it
to be. Most of us are well aware of this fact.
So when we complain that things aren't going
the way we would like them to, we only annoy
those around us, while further darkening our
own mood.

The more we whine and criticize, the smaller
and more unpleasant we become.

Today, instead of complaining about negative
things, I will praise positive things.

Parenting

"Be gentle with the young."

JUVENAL

We live in a fast-paced, demanding world. We expect a lot from others, and they expect a lot from us. This is fine for the world of adults, but it can be a problem when we force similar high expectations onto children.

While it's important to teach children how to behave properly and get along with others, and to keep them active and stimulated, we should never forget that they are still children, with tender hearts and minds.

I sometimes get impatient with children. Today, I will make a special effort to react to them with gentleness rather than impatience.

Group action

> *"Never doubt that a small group of thoughtful,*
> *committed citizens can change the world.*
> *Indeed, it is the only thing that ever has."*
> 🙠 MARGARET MEAD 🙡

The problems of the world—or even the problems of our local community—can seem overwhelming. How can we make a difference? Alone, it's difficult to make significant change; but when we work with others, even on a small scale, the chances that we can make a difference increase dramatically.

A collaboration between parents and teacher can do much more to improve a school that any single parent acting alone. A block association can do much more to improve a neighborhood than any single resident acting alone.

I don't have to feel that I need to tackle every problem in the world by myself. There are many others who care about the same things I do.

Virtues

> **"***Courage is the ladder on which all the other virtues mount.* **"**
>
> ❧CLARE BOOTHE LUCE❧

We like to think of ourselves as being basically good people—people with high values, people who do the right thing. And most of the time, we probably are.

But if we lie because we're afraid to take responsibility for something we've done—if we remain silent when we hear sexist, racist, or other types of hurtful comments—if we fail to act when we see injustice—how virtuous are we really? It takes courage to live our virtues and make them real.

I won't put my values aside simply because it makes my life easier.

februaryの8

Avoiding cynicism

> *"Never be a cynic, even a gentle one.*
> *Never help out a sneer, even at the devil."*
> **❧ VACHEL LINDSAY ❧**

Cynicism is the conversational tone of today's world. We think ourselves clever or hip if we can come up with a quick negative response to the world around us.

We weren't born with this point of view. Children tend naturally to greet the world with openness and positivity, even if they've suffered a number of disappointments. One of the reasons we enjoy being around children is their fresh, upbeat, indefatigable approach to life.

I will "look on the bright side" today, eschewing the snappy but cynical comments I often find so easy to make.

Creating ourselves

"The self is not something ready-made, but something in continuous formation through choice of action."

JOHN DEWEY

We make choices every day that define who we are and what we value. How we dress. What we eat. The kind of car we drive. The quality of work we do. Where we live. What we do with our spare time. How we treat other people. How we treat ourselves.

We need to make those choices carefully and thoughtfully because this is how we create who we are.

I will think hard about the choices I make today and what they say about me as a person.

Learning from mistakes

"*Mistakes are the portals of discovery.*"
JAMES JOYCE

Oh, how we hate making mistakes! They embarrass us, they slow us down, they make us feel stupid or incompetent.

But we would never learn anything new if we didn't make mistakes. A life without mistakes (if such a thing were even possible) would be stagnant, boring, and unproductive. Mistakes open doors to possibilities we would otherwise have never known existed.

Next time I make a mistake (and it could be any moment now), I'll remind myself that there's something good I can learn from it.

Imagining the future

> "*We need men who can dream of things that never were.*"
>
> **JOHN F. KENNEDY**

Can we imagine a building that has never been built? A song that has never been sung? A way of treating a disease that has never been cured?

Luckily, there are those among us who can take such leaps of imagination—and bring the rest of us along with them. How many commonplace things in our lives today would have seemed like miracles just a few decades ago? The microwave oven, the personal computer, the Internet, the cell phone, minimally invasive surgery.

I am thankful for those people who have been able to dream of things that never were and make them real. I will try to do some dreaming myself.

Deciding to be happy

"*Most folks are about as happy as they make up their minds to be.***"**

ABRAHAM LINCOLN

"I'd be happy if only . . ." There's always something we're waiting for—the right relationship, the right job, the right living situation; a child, a raise, a change of seasons—to make us happy.

When we look around, though, we see plenty of people who are happy even without any of the things we want. They simply decide to be happy now, rather than postponing their happiness for a time that may never come.

Happiness is a state of mind, not a set of circumstances. I can—and will—choose to be happy today.

Sharing with friends

> *"Friendship makes prosperity more shining and lessens adversity by dividing and sharing it."*
> ✄ CICERO ✄

When something wonderful happens to us, it may not seem real until we can tell our friends about it. Their happiness for us deepens and intensifies our pleasure.

When something bad happens to us, we search out our friends for comfort, understanding, and assurance. Their sympathy eases our pain and gives us hope.

Knowing how much friendship means to us, how can we be better friends to others in their times of prosperity and adversity?

I will be the best friend I can be to the people who bring so much into my life.

Love

"Who, being loved, is poor?"
 ~ OSCAR WILDE ~

The Beatles sang that money can't buy us love.
It's true. Love is its own sort of wealth, more
precious than any material wealth. And if we
were to sit down and really tally this wealth, we
might be surprised at how well off we are. The
love of a spouse or partner, of family members
and friends—these accounts can quickly add
up.

One thing we have to remember, though:
Love is like friendship. We can't expect to
receive it unless we're willing to give it in kind.

I will say "I love you" at least once today. And I'll
mean it.

Forgiving

❝*Life is an adventure in forgiveness.*❞
🙟NORMAN COUSINS🙞

People are by nature flawed. There will always be times when we do things that are disappointing or hurtful to others. Sometimes these things are done on purpose; sometimes by accident. In either case, the result is the same: someone feels wronged.

It's tempting to hold on to these feelings of being wronged and to harbor grudges. But since we're as likely to wrong as be wronged, wouldn't the world be a better place if we could forgive others as we would like them to forgive us?

I will try to forgive someone who has wronged me.

Reaching our goals

"A goal without a plan is just a wish."
ANTOINE DE SAINT-EXUPÉRY

If we ask people about their goals in life, we may get quick and precise responses—to find a certain kind of employment, to start a business, to learn to play an instrument, to retire early. But many of those same people may have no idea how they will accomplish their goals.

Having goals is important. Without goals, we don't know where we're headed. But having a goal is easy; planning to achieve it is the hard part. What's the first step? How long will it take to reach the goal? What kinds of effort will we need to make? How likely is success? Who can help?

I'll choose one of my goals and lay out a plan to accomplish it, step by step.

Spirituality in action

"The fact that I can plant a seed and it becomes a flower, share a bit of knowledge and it becomes another's, smile at someone and receive a smile in return, are to me continual spiritual exercises."

❧ LEO BUSCAGLIA ❧

We can express our spirituality in many different ways and in many different places and times. We don't have to wait until we're at a place of formal worship to exercise our spirituality. Every moment that we are alive and aware is an opportunity to acknowledge and express our connection to other people and to the world.

I will be open to experiences with other people and with nature today, recognizing the miracle of life and my place in it.

Awakening

> "*There is only one time when it is essential to awaken. That time is now.*"
>
> ❦ BUDDHA ❦

Even with our eyes open, we sometimes go through our days as if we're sleepwalking. These are the only days we have; we need to be aware of them.

I will be awake, really awake, today.

Kind words

"*One kind word can warm three winter months.***"**
❧JAPANESE PROVERB❧

It's easy to say something nice—and even easier to neglect to do so. We glow when someone tells us how much they appreciate something we've done, even if what we've done is as inconsequential as holding open a door or picking up litter. But in our busy daily rush, we don't always think to pass such kindnesses on to others.

I will offer kind words to others as often as I can.

Absurdity

> *"Humor is our way of defending ourselves from life's absurdities by thinking absurdly about them."*
> **❧ LEWIS MUMFORD ☙**

There's almost nothing that can't be helped with a healthy dose of humor. We could rail in anger and frustration about our relationships, work, politics, or the world in general. But it's a lot more fun—and more useful—to laugh instead.

Taking life with a dose of humor can relieve stress, improve mood, help us cope with change, and put things into clearer perspective.

Instead of becoming annoyed today, I will look for the humor in whatever it is that is threatening to irritate me.

A full life

"*One ought, every day at least, to hear a little song, read a good poem, see a fine picture and, if possible, speak a few reasonable words.*"
❧JOHANN WOLFGANG VON GOETHE☙

There are many simple, wonderful experiences readily accessible to us everyday. A few minutes listening to a favorite piece of music, reading a favorite book, or writing in a journal can be more pleasurable and fulfilling than activities requiring much more extravagant expenditures of our time and money.

I will allow myself a few moments of pleasure and peace today. Maybe I'll visit a museum. Or maybe I'll listen to music. Whatever I do, I'll make sure I experience it fully.

Excuses

"It is better to offer no excuse than a bad one."
GEORGE WASHINGTON

We all make mistakes. The problem isn't so much making mistakes as the lengths to which we sometimes go to defend ourselves when we make them. However deep the hole that making the mistake has put us in, it just gets deeper the more we try to explain ourselves. If we would simply say, "I was wrong" and move on, we wouldn't waste so much of our time and energy, and the people around us would respect us more.

I will try to calmly admit any mistakes I make today . . . and then move on.

Our legacy

"When you were born, you cried and the world rejoiced; live your life so that when you die, the world cries and you rejoice."

WHITE ELK

We may not be rich or famous. And we may not be important to anyone other than our friends and family. Still, that's enough. We each have our own legacy to build.

How would we like our friends and family to remember us? How do they think of us today?

The difference between these two things tells us what we need to do with the time that we have left.

I have just one life in which to bring joy to others around me.

Sharing food

"Sharing food with another human being is an intimate act that should not be indulged in lightly."
❧M.F.K. FISHER❧

Standing at the kitchen counter, we quickly gulp down a cup of coffee and breakfast bar, then rush off to work. Lunch may be a package of processed food we microwave and eat at our desk or an all-too-familiar burger from a fast-food joint. Dinner . . . Do we even have time for dinner?

Event the simplest food can seem like a feast when we set the table, gather friends or family, and sit down together to eat. We share our joys and our concerns as we share our food.

I will make at least one meal today an occasion. I won't skimp on the "service." I'll use a napkin, sit at the table, maybe even light a candle.

Advice

*"Good advice is always certain to be ignored,
but that's no reason not to give it."*

⟶AGATHA CHRISTIE⟶

How many times have we done something stupid and wished that someone would have warned us before we did it? Probably not as many times as we *were* warned beforehand and did something stupid anyway.

We often ignore good advice, but we still need to hear it—and more than once. Sometimes it takes several times before good sense can sink in.

Without being bossy or unpleasant, I will give advice when I think it's important—even if I risk irritating someone I like.

Resilience

"*It's not whether you get knocked down, it's whether you get back up.***"**

◈VINCE LOMBARDI◈

Watch a baby learning to walk. When she first goes from crawling to walking, she's down more than she's up. There may be a few tears, but she quickly bounces back up, ready to try again. The urge to walk, to explore the world in a new way, keeps her going.

Wouldn't it be great if we could maintain this same kind of spirit? A baby doesn't think, "Gee, I fell. Now, I'll never learn to walk." As adults, we sometimes let our failures discourage us. If something goes wrong one time, we think it will always go wrong. We don't get up to take the next step.

I know I'll fail once in a while, but I can learn from my failures. When I try something new that I fear I'll fail at, I'll remind myself that I've succeeded in the past by persisting..

Thoughtful responses

"To a quick question, give a slow answer."
ITALIAN PROVERB

Quick wit is much admired. We're impressed by those who can toss off a clever remark on the spur of the moment, seemingly without effort.

A more thoughtful and reasoned remark takes longer. But it can last longer as well. Wouldn't we rather be admired for our wisdom than for our jokes?

I can stop to think before I answer a question. If I do, what I end up saying is likely to be more useful and true than if I spoke quickly without thinking. And, more importantly, I'm less likely to say something I'll regret.

Keeping busy

> "*Look at a day when you are supremely satisfied at the end. It's not a day when you lounge around doing nothing; it's when you had everything to do, and you've done it.*"
>
> **MARGARET THATCHER**

In our too-busy lives, a day with nothing to do sounds as if it would be heavenly. We could stay in bed until noon, read a book without interruption, watch television for hours at a time, or lie in a hammock listening to the buzz and hum of life in the backyard.

Usually, though, if we stay in bed or read a book for too long, our legs start twitching to get up and move about. There's never anything good on television. And our backs hurt when we try to lie in a hammock.

What can I do that will make me feel I've accomplished something in my free time today? I don't have to paint the house or tune up the car. Going for a walk, baking a loaf of bread, or washing the dishes can be enough.

Keeping it positive

"*A positive attitude may not solve all your problems, but it will annoy enough people |to make it worth the effort.*"

HERM ALBRIGHT

People with negative attitudes are easily annoyed by people with positive attitudes. This may be because they see positivity as an implicit indictment—as if they were being charged with weakness, cowardice, or self-indulgence for giving in to their negativity.

On the other hand, people with positive attitudes rarely seem annoyed by people with negative attitudes. This may be because negative people are such easy targets—there's not much sport in taking them on.

Even with some of the crabbiest people I know—maybe especially with the crabbiest people I know—I'm going to stay positive today. It will be interesting to see how they react.

Self-confidence

"Did you ever see an unhappy horse? Did you ever see a bird that had the blues? One reason why birds and horses are not unhappy is because they are not trying to impress other birds and horses."

✒ DALE CARNEGIE ✒

Our gut is sticking out. Are we wearing the right clothes? The car looks pretty battered. Is it time to get a new one? We said a witty thing at work. Did our coworkers notice?

Some days we act if we're on a stage, performing for an audience. Even when we think we're doing well, we can't be happy until we know what our audience thinks of our performance. The problem is, we can never know for sure before—or even after the fact—what other people are really thinking.

What others think of me matters, but it shouldn't matter as much as what I think of myself.

Nurturing creativity

"Every child is an artist. The problem is how to remain an artist once he grows up."
— PABLO PICASSO

When a child gives us a picture, we ooh and aah and put the picture on the refrigerator in a place of honor, regardless of how expertly the picture was rendered. The child's delight in creating something is celebrated and reinforced without needless criticism.

It would be wonderful if we were just as eager to nurture creativity in ourselves as adults, celebrating the creative act for itself, separately from any judgments about its value or quality.

I will compliment others for their creativity instead of trying to come up with reasons why their ideas aren't as good as they might be.

Having faith

"*Not truth, but faith it is that keeps the world alive.*"

EDNA ST. VINCENT MILLAY

We search for truth throughout our lives, but for many of the things most important to us, we simply have to have faith. We have faith that our relationships with others will work out. We have faith that our best efforts will be rewarded with success. We have faith that others will treat us as we deserve to be treated.

This kind of faith is tested, just as spiritual faith may be tested; but our lives are happier for having such faith.

I need to value truth, but I realize that not everything important can be measured against truth.

Joy in living

"When you arise in the morning, give thanks for the food and for the joy of living. If you see no reason for giving thanks, the fault lies only in yourself."

CHIEF TECUMSEH

Starting the day with a positive thought sets the tone for everything that follows. Instead of focusing on our troubles and worries, we can think about our blessings—how lucky we are to have a warm, dry place to sleep; good food to eat; nice clothes to wear; a job to go to; family and friends to support us; a new day to enjoy; fresh air to breath. And, most of all, how lucky we are just to be alive.

I will take a few minutes when I first wake up to think about the many good things in my life.

The gift of responsibility

"*Few things help an individual more than to place responsibility upon him, and to let him know that you trust him.*"

❧ BOOKER T. WASHINGTON ☙

Ultimately, we learn by doing, not by reading a manual. It can be nerve-racking to let children do the dishes for the first time (What if a dish gets broken?) or stay home alone for the first time (What if something happens?). But children will never learn to do the dishes or develop independence without taking that first step on their own.

It can be hard to give up responsibility. We may fear that others won't be as competent as we are. But unless we want to keep doing everything ourselves, eventually we have to be willing to trust others.

Instead of saying, "Oh, thanks, but I'll do it myself," I will trust someone else to take on the responsibility.

Stepping out of our ruts

" The truth is that our finest moments are most likely to occur when we are feeling deeply uncomfortable, unhappy, or unfulfilled. For it is only in such moments, propelled by our discomfort, that we are likely to step out of our ruts and start searching for different ways or truer answers. "

M. SCOTT PECK

As much as we may dislike being unhappy, discomfort can be a powerful motivation to change our lives. Similarly, too much comfort can lull us into complacency and stagnation.

There is nothing wrong with being comfortable, as long as we don't let it close our eyes and mind. And there's nothing wrong with being uncomfortable, as long as we use our discomfort to make our life better.

If this is a good period of my life, I will enjoy it fully. If this is a difficult time, I'll do what I need to do to get through it and to come out stronger.

Finding others

"*Friendship is born at that moment when one person says to another, 'What! You too? I thought I was the only one.'*"

♠ C.S. LEWIS ♠

Some friendships grow over years. Others form in an instant. The commonality of all these friendships is—well, commonality: the recognition of the special things we share in common. Friends assure us that we are not alone in the world—that, as improbable as it may seem, there are other people with quirks, habits, beliefs, and preferences similar to ours. People who agree with us about politics. People who think our jokes are funny. People who like to eat the same food we do.

I love my friends, and I try to show it. Today, I will talk to at least one friend about how much I value our relationship.

Divine balance

"*So divinely is the world organized that every one of us, in our place and time, is in balance with everything else.*"
JOHANN WOLFGANG VON GOETHE

Whether we believe that our world has a divine order, a natural order, or no order at all, we all must acknowledge that everything in this world is interconnected. This world is our world, the only world we have, and we are in it. Science suggests that something as trivial as the beating of a butterfly's wings in the Amazon can influence the formation of a tornado in Texas. Even our smallest acts can have major effects.

I appreciate the miracle of the world. My life's task is to determine my place in it.

Happiness

"Let us be grateful to people who make us happy; they are the charming gardeners who make our souls blossom."

~ MARCEL PROUST ~

We enjoy our time alone—we almost never have enough of it. But there is something wonderful about time spent with friends and family we love that can't be matched by our time alone. As we look back over our lives, it's hard to recall a moment of great happiness that wasn't at least partly due to the fact that we were sharing it with a loved one. How much better our lives would be if we always kept those who make us happy close to us.

I will hug a loved one today, and as I do I'll think how happy I am that this person is part of my life.

Thoughts of change

"*Change your thoughts and you change your world.*"

~NORMAN VINCENT PEALE~

There's no great mystery behind the power of positive thinking. If we assume before the fact that we can't accomplish something, we almost certainly won't. If we believe that we can, we are much more likely to succeed. At least, we'll make the effort.

We talk ourselves out of interesting opportunities all the time—when we ought to be talking ourselves *into* them.

If I catch a negative thought crossing my mind, I can toss it out and replace it with a more positive one.

The moral of the story

"Everything's got a moral, if only you can find it."

LEWIS CARROLL

Things happen for a reason. And if we don't know what that reason is, we create one. It's part of what makes us human—this need to explain things, to feel that there is logic, rationality, and order to the world.

Some of the reasons we come up with for why things happen are thoughtful; others are silly. Some are possible; others are improbable. More important than coming up with the right reason, though, is respecting the impulse that drives us to look for meaning in our lives.

What can I learn from things that happen to me? I'll look for the moral of my own stories.

Following our feelings

"I pay no attention whatever to anybody's praise or blame. I simply follow my own feelings."
WOLFGANG AMADEUS MOZART

We have good instincts about many things. Time and experience have taught us lessons about what we like and don't like, what works and doesn't work, what is true and not true.

We need to trust our intuition. Yes, there will be times when we make mistakes despite our best instincts. But these mistakes add to our experience, hone our instincts, and help us make even better choices the next time.

Before I listen to what everyone else thinks I should do, I'll take some time to figure out how I feel about the situation. Maybe I will need the help of others, but I don't need to follow what others think.

Nature's beauty

"*The best remedy for those who are afraid, lonely or unhappy is to go outside, somewhere where they can be quiet, alone with the heavens, nature and God. Because only then does one feel that all is as it should be and that God wishes to see people happy, amidst the simple beauty of nature.*"

—ANNE FRANK—

A sunny day, a light breeze, a temperature perfect for sitting outside without a jacket— such days make us feel happy, at peace with the world, grateful.

But walking in the rain, making snow angels, or watching the wind whip the trees also can make us feel happy. Nature keeps us grounded in what's real. Winter balances summer, giving the land time to renew itself. Wind sends seeds flying, to give birth to new plants in other places.

If I find myself feeling grouchy, I will get up from my chair and take a quick walk. I will look for signs of nature's beauty that will cheer me.

Blessings to come

"*Give thanks for unknown blessings already on their way.*"
☙ NATIVE AMERICAN PROVERB ❧

We're pretty good at counting our blessings and being grateful for all the wonderful gifts life has bestowed upon us.

It takes a certain amount of faith to be thankful for blessings we haven't received yet—faith that the world is bountiful and generous enough to keep giving to us as long as we live; faith that we will be able to recognize and appreciate our blessings whenever and from wherever they may come.

Today, when I count my blessings, I will make a small leap of faith and be grateful in advance for whatever blessings may come my way tomorrow.

The value of friends

"True friendship consists not in the multitude of friends, but in their worth and value."

꧁ BEN JONSON ꧂

We like to be the life of the party, to have a calendar filled with social events, to have many friends clamoring for our attention. We like to feel wanted, and the more people who seem to like us, the better.

Still, we recognize who our true friends are—and we don't have so many of these. They are the friends who don't wait to ask what they can do when we need help. They're the friends who tell us the things we don't want to hear, but need to hear anyway. They're the friends who know us—in both our good and bad moments—and love us as we are.

I am lucky in having true friends. I will be a true friend as well.

Opening a hand

"You can't shake hands with a clenched fist."
INDIRA GANDHI

We sometimes have to act polite towards a person we dislike or who has hurt us. So we put on a fake smile and do what we need to do to make things okay.

Instead of putting on a fake smile, though, what if we tried smiling for real? Is there something we might like about this person if given a chance? Do we really have a good reason to dislike the person in the first place?

Maybe we won't become great friends. But we'll never know unless we open ourselves to the possibility.

The next time I encounter someone I don't particularly like, I will be genuinely interested in what the person thinks and says. This may show me a new side of the person.

A sense of humor

❝*A sense of humor is part of the art of leadership, of getting along with people, of getting things done.*❞

🙟 DWIGHT D. EISENHOWER 🙝

Being able to laugh at ourselves and the situations we find ourselves in is a highly desirable quality. We don't need to conceal our sense of humor in our public life, keeping it under wraps until we're safely surrounded by family and friends. The ability to approach problems with equanimity and good humor makes things easier not only for ourselves, but also for anyone else lucky enough to be part of our life.

Stand-up comics can make the most ordinary things seem funny. I don't have to be this clever, but if I can see the humor in everyday life, I'm going to be a much better companion to myself and others.

Making decisions

"Never cut a tree down in the wintertime. Never make a negative decision in the low time. Never make your most important decisions when you are in your worst moods. Wait. Be patient. The storm will pass. The spring will come."

❧ROBERT H. SCHULLER☙

When things are going wrong, we want to change them right away. So we buy something that we don't really need. Or we throw away something that we do really need. Or we decline an opportunity because we're afraid that something else might go wrong. Or we make the same mistake again, thinking we'll do better this time.

If I'm in a bad mood, I will put off making important decisions until my outlook and judgment improve.

Trying to be happy

"If only we'd stop trying to be happy, we'd have a pretty good time."

❧ EDITH WHARTON ☙

We can spend a lot of time, money, and energy trying to make ourselves happy—eating fancy meals, going on expensive vacations, throwing big parties, buying nice clothes. We think these things will bring us happiness, but often our happiness is short-lived, lasting about as long as it takes to get heartburn from eating too much, return to work from vacation, clean up after the party, or realize that we don't look as nice in our clothes as we'd hoped we would.

If we could learn to find happiness from moment to moment in the small things of life, we'd always have a pretty good time.

I don't need something outside of myself to make me happy. Happiness is a choice I can make under almost any circumstances.

Friends' recognition

"The best mirror is an old friend."
➤ GEORGE HERBERT ➤

Those who've known us the longest can tell us the truth about ourselves—even when it's truth we might not want to hear. They see us clearly— the good and the bad—and they recognize when we are being phony or overly impressed with ourselves. We need to see our true selves reflected this way.

I'm lucky to have longtime friends who know me and aren't afraid to tell me the truth about myself.

Perspective

"We are all something, but none of us are everything."

◦BLAISE PASCAL◦

Do we think too much of ourselves—or too little? We may have tendencies towards one end of the spectrum or the other. Or we may go back and forth between two extremes, convinced of our importance one day and our insignificance the next.

We all have a place in the world that is significant; we all matter. The trick is not to think that we matter more than anyone else in the world.

I can be happy with my place in the world, without distorting it one way or another.

Our potential

“*There are admirable potentialities in every
human being. Believe in your strength and your
youth. Learn to repeat endlessly to yourself,
'It all depends on me.'*”

ANDRÉ GIDE

Young or not, we can believe in ourselves and in
our ability to get things done. The alternative—
to be convinced that whatever we do makes no
difference—gets us nowhere.

Positive self-talk, like that of the locomotive
in *The Little Engine That Could* ("I think I can, I
think I can"), can be surprisingly effective. Just
as surprising is how often we forget this.

I will keep telling myself that I can make things
happen, that what I do is important, until I
believe it.

Doing our best

66*'I have done my best.' That is about all the
philosophy of living one needs.*99

>LIN YUTANG<

We don't always do our best. Sometimes we
rush through an unpleasant task, put in a half-
hearted effort on a menial task, or fail to finish a
task we weren't required to do. We know when
we're not doing our best, and it tends to make
us feel bad.

Our lives are very complicated. Maybe we
can't always do things perfectly. But we can try
to do our best, even if we're the only ones who
know it.

I may not always be able to do things as well as I
would like, but I can still try to do the best I can,
given the time and priorities I have.

The cost of anger

"Anger can be an expensive luxury."

ITALIAN PROVERB

Ever notice how many mistakes we make when we let ourselves get angry? We drop a dish while cleaning the kitchen, back the car into a pole while we're trying to park, yell at a person who didn't do anything wrong. Such mistakes just make us angrier—only now we're angry at ourselves as well.

We can decide not to be angry in the first place, or we can release our anger as quickly as possible. This doesn't mean that we have to let others take advantage of us. It simply means putting things in perspective so we can act calmly and constructively rather than angrily.

I don't have to get angry, even if it seems justified. Instead, I can think about why I'm upset, whether there's something useful to do about it, and what steps to take next.

Politeness and friendship

"It is wise to apply the oil of refined politeness to the mechanisms of friendship."

— COLETTE —

Friends are the people we can just kick back with. We don't have to treat them special; they'll love us anyway. So we take them for granted. No need to clean up, watch our language, or listen to them respectfully. That's the kind of stuff we save for the people we don't know very well.

Why is it we so often treat the people closest to us with the least care? We're polite to the waitress who brings us coffee, but we can't spare a happy smile for our best friend because we're in a bad mood.

I'll experiment with treating my closest friends just as nicely as I treat the many strangers and casual acquaintances in my life. My friends may be surprised at my sudden politeness, but I'll bet they like it.

Positive attitude

"A strong positive mental attitude will create more miracles than any wonder drug."

~ PATRICIA NEAL ~

We don't understand entirely why positive thoughts impact our bodies in positive ways; we just know that they do. Research has shown that people who are sick improve more quickly when they have a positive attitude rather than a negative attitude. And we all know the power of the placebo effect.

A positive attitude by itself may not cure an illness, but at the very least it helps us cope better. If a positive attitude can help us when we're sick, how might it benefit us when we're not sick?

I can face whatever comes today with a positive attitude.

High aspirations

"*Far away there in the sunshine are my highest aspirations. I may not reach them, but I can look up and see their beauty, believe in them, and try to follow them.*"

❧LOUISA MAY ALCOTT☙

We set simple goals for what we need to do today or this week, writing them on a to-do list: buy groceries, pick up the dry cleaning, wash the car. It feels good to accomplish these things, but they aren't the kinds of goals by which we hope to define our legacy.

Our long-term goals should reflect our highest aspirations—goals that we can reach only if we stretch ourselves, do the best we can, and be the best that we can be.

I will write down my long-term goals and put the list where I can see it easily to remind me of what I hope to accomplish in my life.

Being satisfied

> "*You can never get enough of what you don't need to make you happy.*"
> — ERIC HOFFER —

More. We always want more. More possessions, more money, more popularity—whatever it is we think we don't have enough of. If we just had more, we'd be happy.

We should know better. If what we have of something right now isn't giving us any happiness, why should more of it give us happiness? More of nothing is still nothing.

Today I will find satisfaction in things I already have. Before I look for more of something, I'll make sure that it is something I know brings me happiness.

Dancing every day

"Every day brings a chance for you to draw in a breath, kick off your shoes, and dance."
      ❧ OPRAH WINFREY ❧

When opportunity presents itself, we need to be willing to stand up, take a breath, and commit ourselves to it wholeheartedly, even at the risk of looking a little silly. Life is short. Let's engage it as passionately as we can.

I want to dance today. And so I will. Maybe I'll dance by myself, or maybe I'll grab someone I love and have them dance with me.

Trust

"It is better to suffer wrong than to do it, and happier to be sometimes cheated than not to trust."

❧SAMUEL JOHNSON☙

We worry about being taken advantage of, so we keep our guard up. We protect ourselves. We're suspicious of people we don't know very well.

It's good to be careful. There are people who would cheat us if they could. But being cheated is not the worst thing that can happen to us. Worse would be to let our mistrust make us bitter, cold, and withdrawn.

I am smart about protecting myself, but I want to be open to people and experiences as well.

Changing our lives

"*Human beings, by changing the inner attitudes of their minds, can change the outer aspects of their lives.*"

❧ WILLIAM JAMES ❧

Some call it visioning. Others call it dreaming, reframing, visualization, positive thinking, or cognitive therapy. And still others just do it and don't call it anything. It's the art of deliberately picturing something that we desire—a behavior, goal, or outcome—so that it's more likely to come about.

Thinking alone isn't going to make something happen, of course. But once we have a vision, we can begin to act in ways that will make the vision become real.

I have a picture of how I want my life to go. What do I need to do to make it happen?

Hope

"Hope costs nothing."

❧ COLETTE ❧

The last thing we should ever lose is hope, even in the face of the impossible. It costs us nothing to hope. And without hope we are certain to fail.

Without hope, we can't move. We sit and wait for what we believe is inevitable. We may never know for sure whether we could have changed things; all we know is that we didn't even try.

I can hope for the best—and let that hope tell me what I need to do to make it happen.

Self-reliance

"Chop your own wood and it will warm you twice."
❧ HENRY FORD ❧

We can all use help, at home and at work. But we appreciate our clean house more when we've cleaned it ourselves, and we enjoy eating more when we've planned, prepared, and served the food ourselves.

It's very satisfying to do things ourselves when we can—and it reminds us that we are competent, useful people, no matter how much or how little we have.

What task that I might normally skip or give to someone else can I take on today? Maybe instead of putting dishes in the dishwasher, I can enjoy the experience of washing them by hand. Or I can mow my own lawn, pull my own weeds.

Being in harmony

"*Happiness is when what you think, what you say, and what you do are all in harmony.*"

MAHATMA GANDHI

Living in a way that reflects our beliefs should be easy, but we slip all the time. We believe in honesty, but fib to avoid getting in trouble. We believe in kindness, but duck around the corner to avoid someone we don't have time to talk to.

Doing what we can to "walk the talk" doesn't just make us better people; it makes us happier people as well. We don't have to think hard about how we're going to react to something or what the right action is, when we follow our own beliefs.

I have strong beliefs, and I will live my beliefs as best I can. This means making sure that what I think, what I say, and what I do are the same thing.

Tact

> "*Tact is the knack of making a point without making an enemy.*"
>
> ~ SIR ISAAC NEWTON ~

When we're right, we're right—and we want everyone to know it. Funny how others roll their eyes and cough a little behind their hands when we tell them just what we think. Discouraging how they don't agree with us right away.

There's no problem with having strong opinions—it shows that we care about things. But if we wield our opinions like clubs, we will never convince anyone that our opinions are right.

When I'm in a conversation with others, I can tell them clearly what I think without being pushy about it.

Wanting more

66 *It is not the man who has too little, but the man who craves more, that is poor.* 99

SENECA

How many things do we need to make us happy? Fewer than we think. In fact, doesn't it sometimes seem like the more "stuff" we have, the less happy we feel? More stuff means more that we have to take care of, more that can suddenly go wrong on us, more clutter around us.

We can't get everything we think we want, but we can readjust our thinking to find happiness in the riches we already have.

It's a good day to count my blessings, rather than the number of blessings I wish I had.

Doing what we can

> *"If you can't feed a hundred people, then just feed one."*
>
> ❧ MOTHER TERESA ❧

It's easy to feel overwhelmed by bad news in the world. How can we possibly help when the problems seem so big?

Instead of becoming discouraged about how much needs to be done, we can focus on what is doable, however limited this may seem. One hour a week tutoring a new immigrant. A donation to an organization that provides services to those in need. A casserole for a sick friend. A phone call to a lonely senior.

If one hundred of us feed just one hungry person each, a hundred people will be fed.

What can I do today—even one small thing—to help someone in need?

Prosperity

"*Prosperity is only an instrument to be used, not a deity to be worshiped.*"

CALVIN COOLIDGE

Money makes many things easier, no doubt about it. We sleep more soundly when we're not worrying about how we're going to pay our bills.

Where we go wrong is not in having money, but in thinking that money is what defines our worth. We take a job we're not crazy about because of the money. We think the man down the block must be smart and important because he has more money than we do.

I can think about money as something that helps me do good things for myself and others, not as a goal in itself.

Near to happiness

"To be kind to all, to like many and love a few,
to be needed and wanted by those we love, is
certainly the nearest we can come to happiness."
MARY ROBERTS RINEHART

There is no great mystery to being happy.
Happiness is within easy reach of us all, though
we don't always appreciate this fact.

The secret to happiness is this: Treat others
as you would like to be treated. That's about
it. Like a stick thrown to a dog, love and kindness keep coming back. When we make others
happy, we make ourselves happy.

I have a good life, with friends I love and who love
me.

Facing the consequences

> ❝*You can do anything in this world if you are*
> *prepared to take the consequences.*❞
> ∽ W. SOMERSET MAUGHAM ∽

What holds us back isn't necessarily that we
don't know what to do; it's that we worry about
what will happen if we do it. What if people
think we're being silly? What if we make
enemies? What if our idea doesn't work the way
we thought it would?

People who make a difference are those who
understand that taking an action may cause an
equal and opposing reaction—but who take
action anyway.

I am strong enough to handle any negative
reactions when I do what I need to.

Holding back criticism

"Let him who is without sin cast the first stone."
❧ JESUS CHRIST ❧

It's tempting to criticize others. Sometimes we're just gossiping "for fun," and sometimes we are truly offended by what others have said or done.

But we hate to be criticized ourselves. Sure, there may be reasons for others to criticize us. But how could they be so insensitive? So heartless? Don't they realize that we're just ordinary folk trying to do our best? So we're not perfect—so what?

I can be quick to criticize. If there's one thing I could do to be a better person, it would be to be as generous about the flaws and mistakes of others as I am about my own.

Too many details

> **"***Our life is frittered away by detail. . . .***
> ***Simplify, simplify.***"**
> ❧ HENRY DAVID THOREAU ❧

We keep our to-do list handy all the time, filled with one chore after another. At the end of the day, even if we've finished several of these chores, we still don't feel that we've made a much of a dent in our list.

But think about this: If months pass and certain goals still haven't been accomplished, how important could these goals have been to begin with?

The first chore on my to-do list today will be to decide what is important and what isn't, and to begin to simplify my life.

New landscapes

"The real voyage of discovery consists not in seeking new landscapes but in having new eyes."
MARCEL PROUST

When we're on vacation, we have a heightened interest in everything around us. Our eyes are wide open. We try new things and visit new places. We are upbeat and optimistic.

At home, we take many things for granted. Habit blinds us to discoveries that lie right before our eyes. We may never visit attractions that outsiders travel miles to see. We miss out on all sorts of opportunities because we're simply not looking for them.

For fun, I will pretend to be a tourist in my own town. What would someone visiting for the first time see that I take for granted?

Interests vs. beliefs

"One person with a belief is equal to a force of ninety-nine who have only interests."
JOHN STUART MILL

When we really put our heart and soul into something, we're unstoppable. We do this when we truly believe. Maybe we believe that a candidate we support will make a real difference, that our work can change people's lives for the better, that a particular religious principle in important.

When we're acting with passion, we do what we need to do, without getting discouraged or giving up. And we inspire others to join us.

I can support my beliefs with action, even when it feels like I'm in the minority. Especially when it feels like I'm in the minority.

Experience and character

"Character cannot be developed in ease and quiet. Only through experience of trial and suffering can the soul be strengthened, ambition inspired, and success achieved."

HELEN KELLER

We may wish for an easier life at times, but we know that the way we handle ourselves in the difficult periods is what truly shapes who we are. The people we admire the most aren't those who've had everything given to them. They are the people who have had to work hard and even suffer to achieve what they have achieved.

I can handle life's tragedies and setbacks. I don't welcome these events, but I recognize that they have much more to do with defining my character than happy times do.

Life worth living

"It's faith in something and enthusiam for
something that makes life worth living."
OLIVER WENDELL HOLMES

A cynical, aloof, done-it-all approach to life isn't sophisticated; it's actually kind of sad. Some people act as if the world were much too boring and dull for them to get excited about it. But, whatever their pretensions, their attitude, in the end, makes them boring and dull.

What's the fun in being with someone who can't get excited about anything, who doesn't seem to care about anything?

I will allow myself to be enthusiastic about the world, whether others think it's cool or not.

Entertaining friends

"*The ornament of a house is the friends who frequent it.*"
RALPH WALDO EMERSON

We may hesitate to invite company over because we worry that our house is a mess or we don't cook well enough or our new furniture is too shabby. We've forgotten that the reason friends come to our house is not because we live like royalty. It's because they like us and enjoy our company.

Every house is cozy and attractive when it's filled with friends enjoying themselves.

No more excuses. I will plan a get-together with friends at my house for the near future.

Tenderness and passion

"*Tenderness is greater proof of love than the most passionate of vows.*"

MARLENE DIETRICH

We watch a lot of movies in which love is shown by big gestures, the perfect words, intense passion. Why aren't our own love lives like this?

Tenderness doesn't translate all that well to the big screen. Too subtle, too private, not enough dramatic tension. But we don't live in the movies. We live in the real world, where someone who can always tell when we really need a hug is a better partner than someone who swings down from the ceiling to, literally, sweep us off our feet.

I appreciate the small things my partner does to show how much I am loved and cared for.

Unlikely happiness

"*My life has no purpose, no direction, no aim, no meaning, and yet I'm happy. I can't figure it out. What am I doing right?*"

❧ CHARLES SCHULZ ☙

Some days we just feel good for no particular reason. Let's not pick this feeling apart and analyze it away. Let's just enjoy it.

If I feel good, I'm going to count myself lucky and have a great day.

Spiritual happiness

"I never thought that a lot of money or fine clothes—the finer things of life—would make you happy. My concept of happiness is to be filled in a spiritual sense."

        ◆CORETTA SCOTT KING◆

We know that the so-called finer things of life don't provide us with the same satisfactions as the more spiritual things in life: a beautiful spring day, a child's love, a starry night. Yet we spend a lot of our time in stores, stocking up on things that can't fulfill us.

Where do we go to be filled in a spiritual sense? For some, this would be a church or similar place of worship. But spirituality can be experienced anywhere, public or private.

I like my clothes, and money is nice, but I want to recognize and encourage my spiritual side. This may mean attending a place of worship. Or it may mean setting aside a few moments for myself each day to calmly reflect on my life.

Improving ourselves

"*There's only one corner of the universe you can be certain of improving, and that's your own self.*"
ALDOUS HUXLEY

We've got all kinds of ideas for how the world could be better, and we're usually more than happy to share them with anyone who wants to listen—and even those who don't. How the government ought to be run. How local merchants ought to operate their businesses. How our best friends ought to lead their lives.

If we applied these ideas to our own lives, not only might we improve ourselves, but we might also realize that we don't have as many answers as we think we do.

My ideas are good ones, but there's no reason anyone else should listen to them. They have their own ideas about how things should be done, and I can respect this.

Patience

"Patience is the companion of wisdom."
　　　　❧ ST. AUGUSTINE ❧

We live in an impatient world. We tap our feet nervously, bite our lips, jiggle the keys in our hand. We don't like to wait, and we don't wait gracefully.

When something is bothering us, we want the answer *now*, not later. We rush into solutions that we haven't thought out well.

Wisdom is like bread dough. It needs time to rise.

I don't expect everything to happen right this moment, even though I sometimes wish it would.

Talking instead of doing

"A meowing cat catches no mice."

YIDDISH PROVERB

Talk, talk, talk. Sometimes we spend more time talking about what we want to do than actually doing it. We may need reassurance that we're on the right track, or we're hoping for someone to give us advice. Or we just find it easier to talk than to actually take that first step.

I'll make sure that I'm actually doing things, not just talking about doing them.

Quiet

"Never be afraid to sit awhile and think."
LORRAINE HANSBURY

Hustle and bustle are part of our lives. We live with constant background noise: the sounds of human activity on the one hand—cars, aircraft, heavy machinery, music players—and the sounds of the natural world on the other—birds, insects, wind, thunder.

We rarely get the chance to experience quiet—and when we do, we often behave as if we're afraid of it. No one home? Quick, turn on the television. A few moments in the car? Search for something on the radio. Going for a walk? Plug in the earphones and listen to music.

Once in a while, we need to embrace silence.

Quiet is a luxury that costs me nothing. I can take a few moments each day to simply sit and think, without the need of any foreground or background noise.

Victory and defeat

> "*More people are ruined by victory, I imagine, than by defeat.*"
>
> ❧ELEANOR ROOSEVELT❧

Bad losers are hard to take—but not nearly as hard to take as bad winners. If we assume that we are somehow better than everyone else and more deserving of victory, we can turn victory into disaster.

Maybe we did pay our dues and work hard. But there is always some luck in every victory. And for all we know, our opponents worked even harder than we did.

Remember this: Defeat has a way of focusing thought and motivation. If we don't learn from our victories as much as we learn from our defeats, we may not be so lucky next time.

I like to win, and it's okay to celebrate when I do. But I must remember that winning doesn't make me better than others.

More than we need

"A human being has a natural desire to have more of a good thing than he needs."

MARK TWAIN

Set a great meal down in front of us, and we'll eat well past the point of being full. It's hard to say, "That's enough," when something looks and tastes so good.

Experience should tell us, though, that when we're eating too much the last bites don't taste nearly as good as the first ones—and that after the meal we will feel bloated, heavy, and even a little nauseated. Stopping while we're still enjoying a meal takes some discipline, but leaves us with a much better experience.

I know when I've had enough of anything, whether it's food or a shopping trip or a party. I'll stop before I've had too much.

Giving time

> *"You must give some time to your fellow men. Even if it's a little thing, do something for others—something for which you get no pay but the privilege of doing it."*
> **ALBERT SCHWEITZER**

People honor us when they allow us to help them. It shows trust—trust that we will not look down upon them for being weak or needy, trust that we will not hold them in our debt.

There is no gift too small to matter—no gift that doesn't give back to us as much as it gives to others.

I can do something for another person today. It doesn't have to be a big thing. A small gesture can be all that is needed to make a difference.

Who we are

"*It's where we go, and what we do when we get there, that tells us who we are.*"
❧ JOYCE CAROL OATES ❧

We make choices every day about where we go. Sometimes big choices, like where to spend a vacation or to buy a house. But mostly small choices: Where will we get coffee today? Buy a pair of socks? Load up on groceries?

Even these ordinary choices say something about who we are. Do we shop at exclusive shops, at local family-owned stores, at chain discount stores, at co-ops? These choices are not "right" or "wrong," but they do say something about our values.

I will pay attention to where I conduct my daily business and where I go to relax and entertain myself. Do my choices truly reflect my values?

Limits

> *"One cannot collect all the beautiful shells on the beach."*
> **ANNE MORROW LINDBERGH**

When we consider all the rich possibilities of the world, our desire knows no limits. A summer home in the mountains, a romantic getaway to an exotic island, an advanced degree from a prestigious university—so many possibilities, so little time.

We can, however, enjoy the things we do experience as completely as possible. We don't need to do everything we can imagine to have a full life.

(Even if we could collect all the beautiful shells on the beach, what appeal would the beach then hold for us?)

I have had wonderful experiences. I am lucky.

Providing the flame

66*Any committee is only as good as the most knowledgeable, determined, and vigorous person on it. There must be somebody who provides the flame.*99

❧ LADY BIRD JOHNSON ❧

Every gathering needs at least one person to be the spark to get things going. Whether we're at a party, the office, or a neighborhood meeting, we need someone to focus and energize the group.

A single negative person can also put out that spark—if we stand by and let it happen. Instead of responding to negativity with negativity, though, we can choose to help ignite the group once again.

I can be the person who provides the flame if I set my mind to it.

Letting happiness in

"Happiness often sneaks in through a door you didn't know you left open."

❧JOHN BARRYMORE☙

We think we know what makes us happy—watching a favorite television show, going out with a longtime friend, tending our garden. Not surprisingly, we try to make time for the things that bring us happiness.

If we keep ourselves open to it, however, we may find happiness in surprising ways. Can doing dishes make us happy? Think about the warm water and soap suds, the quiet time at the sink while we go over the day's events in our minds, the satisfaction of seeing a pile of dirty dishes change to a neatly stacked set of clean dishes, ready for their next use.

I will allow happiness to come to me in ways I least expect.

Loving ourselves

"You, yourself, as much as anybody in the entire universe, deserve your love and affection."

≈ BUDDHA ≈

No one is harder on us than we are on ourselves. We see only our physical flaws when we look in the mirror. We remember only our mistakes when we look back on the day we've just spent. We sometimes beat ourselves up even when we've done nothing wrong.

And yet, others like us. Some even love us. What do they see in us that we don't? It's good to be honest with ourselves, but we also should be kind. We can give more love and affection to others if we start with love and affection for ourselves.

I am a good person, trying to do the best I can. I will remember this and be as nice to myself as I try to be to others.

From failure to success

"Success is the ability to go from one failure to another with no loss of enthusiasm."
☙ SIR WINSTON CHURCHILL ☙

How quickly we can get discouraged. We try something once, it doesn't work, and we give up.

If Thomas Edison had acted this way, we might not have had the light bulb until many years later. If the Wright brothers had given up after a crash or two, plane travel might have been delayed by years. Instead, Edison and the Wright brothers (and countless other innovators throughout history) persisted through their failures until they finally succeeded.

I don't succeed at everything I try, and that's okay. What's important is that I keep trying.

Holy curiosity

*" The important thing is not to stop questioning.
Curiosity has its own reason for existing.
One cannot help but be in awe when he
contemplates the mysteries of eternity, of life, of
the marvelous structure of reality. It is enough
if one tries merely to comprehend a little of this
mystery every day. Never lose a holy curiosity. "*
ALBERT EINSTEIN

No matter what our spiritual beliefs, testing
them against our experience only makes them
deeper and more meaningful.

Our lives, the earth we live on, the vast
universe—all amaze us. We are fortunate to be
here in this time and place. Let us never lose our
curiosity about why we are here and what being
here means.

I look up at the stars in wonder and happiness.
What does it all mean? Each day I try to understand the answer to this question.

Our responsibility

" *Treat the earth well.*
  It was not given to you by your parents,
  It was loaned to you by your children.
  We do not inherit the earth from our ancestors,
  We borrow it from our children. "

NATIVE AMERICAN PROVERB

We are here for a very short time—guests only on this planet, not its owners. And we should act as any good guest would act in someone else's home.

It is our duty to treat the earth well and to leave it in a way that future generations can enjoy what we have enjoyed.

There are many small things I can do to help preserve the earth, from turning the lights off when I leave a room to recycling cans and bottles. These may seem insignificant, but if everyone acted in this way, it would make a big difference.

Work and play

> *"Work and play are words used to describe the same thing under differing conditions."*
>
> ❧ MARK TWAIN ☙

On our best workdays, we can't wait to get up and get started. We arrive with energy and enthusiasm, and we leave, however many hours later, filled with satisfaction. The day seems to fly by in a happy blur.

A job can be soul-crushing, but it doesn't have to be. Even in the worst circumstances, we can bring a positive perspective to our work and strive to be fully engaged.

How can I make my job more satisfying today?

Getting results

"*Both tears and sweat are salty, but they render a different result. Tears will get you sympathy; sweat will get you change.*"

JESSE JACKSON

It takes a lot of energy to whine and complain about how unfair things are—energy we are often too willing to expend.

Maybe we're right. Maybe we really have been treated unfairly. Maybe someone has it in for us. Maybe it's raining on the day we wanted to take a picnic. We'd do better to figure out how to turn this situation into something positive—and we'd annoy our friends a lot less.

If I'm tempted to complain and cry when things don't go my way, I can get myself moving instead. Do I need to work harder, try something different, or just change my plans? Chances are, what I need to do is simple and well within my control.

Simple delights

"Teach us delight in simple things."
RUDYARD KIPLING

We don't need money or fancy toys to have a good time. The world is full of things that can delight us—the sound of a spring robin, the scent of a flower, the smile on a child's face.

I will count the things that delight me today—and I bet I find that most of them are simple things.

Giving comfort

"Grant that we may not so much seek to be consoled as to console. To be understood as to understand."

St. Francis of Assisi

When we can be useful to others, rather than merely hoping that they will be useful to us, we are better people for it. What's more, we are happier.

To understand others, we need to really listen to them rather than make assumptions, or hear with only half our attention because we're eager to make our own points.

People have given me comfort and understanding when I needed it. I hope I can do as well for others.

True religion

"True religion is real living; living with all one's soul, with all one's goodness and righteousness."
ALBERT EINSTEIN

We may or may not belong to an organized religion. We may or may not frequent a place of worship. But if we live our life as fully as we can in accordance with our deepest and most passionate beliefs, then we are truly religious.

I live in a way that honors my religious beliefs.

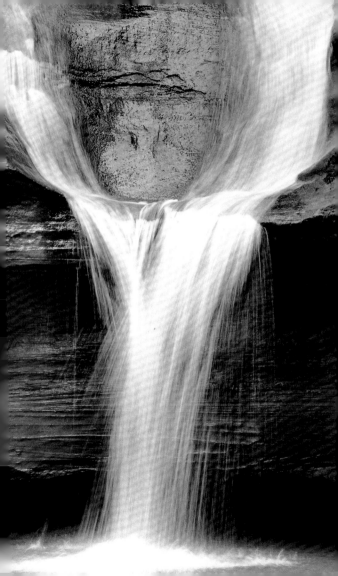

Blame and effort

"*A man can get discouraged many times, but he is not a failure until he begins to blame somebody else and stops trying.*"
JOHN BURROUGHS

Things often don't go the way we'd like them to. Some days it seems as if no matter how hard we work, no matter how many times we get up and try again, we just can't win.

It's not our fault, we think . . . so it must be somebody else's fault. We can spend a lot of time complaining about this, instead of dusting ourselves off and trying yet again.

If I find myself blaming others, I will stop and figure out what I can do instead. Maybe I need a new strategy.

Choosing change

"Things do not change; we change."
❧HENRY DAVID THOREAU❧

In many ways, the world is always only what it is, good and bad. It doesn't change. What changes is the way we look at the world, the way we choose to interact with it.

Recognizing this gives us amazing power. If we can change ourselves—and we can—we can change our relationship with the world.

It's a simple thing to remember: I can change, and when I change, so do my circumstances.

Dreams and action

"To accomplish great things, we must dream as well as act."

ANATOLE FRANCE

We can walk through every day, doing what needs to be done at home and at work. It's not a bad life—and it's the life most of us lead. We leave a legacy of love and effort. There's nothing wrong with this.

But those who are not afraid to dream go beyond this, far beyond this. Their actions follow the path of their dreams. The combination of dreams and action opens the way for amazing advances in science, art, and culture.

I am good at getting things done, but I don't always give myself time to dream. I may not be brilliant, but I will give myself the chance to see what dreaming brings into my life.

What we do

> **"**Where I was born and where and how I have
> lived is unimportant. It is what I have done with
> where I have been that should be of interest. **"**
> — GEORGIA O'KEEFE —

Some people we know are always telling new
acquaintances where they were born, where they
went to college, where they live now, as if these
things were evidence of their importance.

But what have they really done? A degree
from the most prestigious university doesn't
make anyone a success. Being born into a
family of accomplishment may be an advantage,
but it doesn't guarantee success.

If I'm tempted to try to impress someone with my
personal background, I'll stop and ask myself why I
think it matters. Instead of trying to impress with
my history, I will try to let people know who I am
and what I stand for now.

Doing for others

"There is nothing to make you like other human beings so much as doing things for them."

>ᴢᴏʀᴀ Nᴇᴀʟᴇ Hᴜʀsᴛᴏɴ

We like ourselves better when we help others, but the astonishing thing is that we also tend to like others better. It is something of a gift when people allow us to help them. We appreciate the givers of this gift.

I will help others and realize that they are giving me a gift that I welcome.

Sense of wonder

"If a child is to keep alive his inborn sense of wonder . . . he needs the companionship of at least one adult who can share it, rediscovering with him the joy, excitement, and mystery of the world we live in."

⮞ RACHEL CARSON ⮜

Social research shows us that one of the most important factors for a child becoming a caring, responsible adult is the influence and encouragement of adult mentors. These adults could be parents or other family members, teachers, church leaders—anyone with a sincere interest in the child's success.

Whether or not I have children, I can find a way to help a child succeed. I can join a volunteer organization. I can tutor a neighbor's child or coach an after-school team. There are many things I could do to make a real difference in a young person's life.

A well-spent life

"As a well-spent day brings happy sleep, so life well used brings happy death."
LEONARDO DA VINCI

It feels so good to snuggle into our bed at the end of a busy day. We're satisfied with the work we've done and our interactions with those we care about. We've left the world a slightly better place than it was when we got up in the morning. And now we sink into a well-deserved and wonderful sleep.

This simple day makes a great model for a worthwhile life as well. Can we leave the world better than when we came into it?

If every day I try to make some small but important difference in the world, my life will have mattered a great deal.

Moderation

❝*Moderation. Small helpings. Sample a little bit of everything. These are the secrets of happiness and good health.*❞

🠶 JULIA CHILD 🠴

We can indulge ourselves, enjoy the things we really like—the best chocolate, a perfect steak—and still exercise moderation. One bite of the best chocolate tastes much better than a pound of ordinary chocolate. In fact, it tastes better than a pound of any kind of chocolate. Too much and we feel a little ill—and angry with ourselves. One bite, slowly melting on the tongue, and we enjoy every moment of it.

The idea of moderation as a principle for a happy life is an ancient philosophy, but it still makes sense.

I don't have to deprive myself—I shouldn't deprive myself. I can enjoy my favorite things, as long as I do so with moderation.

Making miracles

"Hope for a miracle. But don't depend on one."
❧TALMUD❧

There's no harm in wishing for miracles to get us out of our worst messes—unless wishing is all that we do. We'd like someone to offer us the perfect job. We want our friends who are ill to recover quickly. We long for the person of our dreams to desire us.

Sometimes miracles do happen, but more often we must be the architects of our own miracles. Instead of waiting to be offered the perfect job, we buckle down and work extra hours. We network and apply ourselves so that when the right position finally does come along, we have a good shot at it.

I can dream of miracles, but I will do what I need to do to make good things happen.

Repairing friendships

> "*If a man does not make new acquaintances as he advances through life, he will soon find himself left alone. A man should keep his friendships in constant repair.*"
>
> ❧ SAMUEL JOHNSON ☙

We have old friends we value greatly; some have known us since we were children. We have friends from high school and from our first job, friends who were at our special events, friends whose parents knew our parents.

We keep these friends—and make new ones—because we are careful to tend to the friendships. We make the phone calls, send the emails, try to get together for a meal. If we haven't heard from someone in a while, we reach out—and we don't try to keep track of who calls more often. The important thing is the friendship.

Is there a friend I haven't talked to in a while? I won't let one more day go by without tending to our relationship.

Win, win

"Joint undertakings stand a better chance when they benefit both sides."

≈ EURIPEDES ≈

We like to win—and so does everyone else. When we do things with other people—whether it's a project at work or planning a vacation with the family—things fall apart quickly if we don't figure out a way for everyone to get something out of it.

To have a win-win situation, we have to understand what those whom we're dealing with want—and that means listening to what they have to say.

I'm more likely to get what I want if I understand what others want and look for solutions that benefit us all.

Developing character

"If you will think about what you ought to do for other people, your character will take care of itself. Character is a by-product, and any man who devotes himself to its cultivation in his own case will become a selfish prig."

WOODROW WILSON

To develop our character we should first aim to do right by others. Being good to others is an action; becoming a good person is a result of this action. If our goal is merely to appear good in the eyes of others, we are acting selfishly. And little good comes from this.

I will devote myself to helping others and not worry about whether I am perceived as a good person. My character will take care of itself if I take care of others.

Judged by our actions

> ❝We judge ourselves by what we feel capable of doing, while others judge us by what we have already done.❞
> ❧HENRY WADSWORTH LONGFELLOW❧

Life is like a permanent job interview. We walk into the interview feeling as if we are capable of doing almost anything—if life would just give us a chance.

But life insists on asking us what we've actually done. A kind person is a person who acts kindly to others. An honest person is a person who tells the truth and is fair with others. Understanding what others see in us can help us become more like the person we perceive ourselves to be.

I wonder what others see when they look at me. I will take a hard look at myself to make sure my actions align with the person I believe I am.

Perfection

> "*He that will have a perfect brother must resign himself to remaining brotherless.*"
>
> **ITALIAN PROVERB**

Why do those closest to us sometimes refuse to act the way we would like them to? Why aren't they always exactly the people we would like them to be?

We have many friends, and, oddly, not one of them is perfect. We love them all, however, as much for, as in spite of, their imperfections. Which is a good thing, for if we demanded perfection we would have no friends.

There's no reason anyone should be perfect just for me. I like my friends and family just the way they are.

Perseverance and confidence

"*Life is not easy for any of us. But what of that?
We must have perseverance and above all
confidence in ourselves. We must believe that we
are gifted for something, and that this thing, at
whatever cost, must be attained.*"

MARIE CURIE

We can come up with a dozen excuses for why
we haven't accomplished more in our life. Not
enough money. Not enough time. Family
obligations. Personal problems. No support.
No opportunities. Bad luck.

Some people do seem to get more breaks than
us; but many start with a lot less and face more
daunting odds, yet somehow persevere.

What goals do I really care about and what can
I do to achieve them—with no excuses or
explanations for why things are difficult?

Making others laugh

"I learned quickly that when I made others laugh, they liked me."

 ART BUCHWALD

We don't have to act like clowns to get others to laugh. We just have to keep our sense of humor and let it show when it's appropriate.

It feels good to see others smile and to hear them laugh—as long as the laughter is genuine, open, and honest, and not mean or derisive. When we feel like poking fun at another person, we should first consider poking fun at ourselves. This may be the easiest way to get people to both like us and laugh with us.

Can I make someone laugh today?

Grief

"Grief is the agony of an instant, the indulgence of grief the blunder of a life."

~ BENJAMIN DISRAELI ~

Loss is painful. It's natural for us to grieve over things we've lost. And it takes time to fill the hole left by a loss. The larger the hole, the longer it takes to fill it.

At some point, though, we need to put painful feelings aside so that we can get on with the business of living. This doesn't mean ignoring or forgetting our loss, but, rather, recognizing that life is a gift that we have a responsibility to honor. We honor what we have lost as well when we learn from our loss, incorporate it into who we are, and move on.

Loss is natural and unavoidable. I understand and accept this.

Achievement and success

“*My mother drew a distinction between achievement and success. She said that achievement is the knowledge that you have studied and worked hard and done the best that is in you. Success is being praised by others. That is nice, but not as important or satisfying. Always aim for achievement and forget about success.*”

✿HELEN HAYES✿

We enjoy it when our work is recognized by others. Our boss tells us we've done a good job. Our friends are impressed by something we've just shown them. A teacher praises an essay we've written.

This kind of recognition helps motivate us, as any good teacher, parent, or boss knows. But when we do our best—whether recognized by others or not—the feeling is better than any compliment or collection of gold stars.

I celebrate my own work when I know I've achieved my best.

Doing a little

"Nobody made a greater mistake than he who did nothing because he could do only a little."

❧ EDMUND BURKE ☙

We put off cleaning the garage because the job seems too big to finish. We refrain from doing anything to help the poor in our community because the need is too great. We don't start a diet because we'll never be able to take off all of our excess weight.

But if we cleaned just one portion of the garage each weekend or made one small donation to a local charity each month or drank one less can of soda each day, before long we would have accomplished a great deal— certainly much more than had we done nothing.

Instead of being overwhelmed by the size of a task in front of me, I will take one small action at a time. These actions add up.

Feeling vs. doing

> *"You cannot make yourself feel something you do not feel, but you can make yourself do right in spite of your feelings."*
>
> ❧PEARL S. BUCK❧

"I just don't feel like it," a child whines—and, sometimes, neither do we. We know what we're supposed to do, but we're afraid to do it or too bored to do it or we think it's going to be too much work.

We assume that good people do the right thing because it's natural to them. That may be true for some, but many of us have to decide to straighten our shoulders, lift our heads up, and do what we know is right even when we might prefer to whine a little, too.

I know what I need to do, even if part of me would rather avoid it. I will do what's right.

Spiritual existence

"*Everything science has taught me—and continues to teach me—strengthens my belief in the continuity of our spiritual existence after death. Nothing disappears without a trace.*"

❧ WERNHER VON BRAUN ☙

Human beings have always attempted to understand what happens after death. Over the centuries people have held many different opinions about whether there is life after death and, if so, what it is like. We can never know with certainty what happens after we die, simply because there is no empirical way to determine it. Whatever we believe is ultimately a matter of faith.

I don't know for sure what will happen to me after I die, but looking for answers helps me become a better person while I'm alive.

Keeping ourselves down

"As long as you keep a person down, some part of you has to be down there to hold him down, so it means you cannot soar as you otherwise might."

❧ MARIAN ANDERSON ❧

Does someone else always have to lose in order for us to win? Sometimes we act as if that's the case. We scheme covertly or overtly, trying to make sure that some rival—for affection, for position, for attention—doesn't get what he or she wants. We drop hints, gossip, hold back information.

But when we try to keep others down, we also keep ourselves down; we become meaner and smaller than our best selves. All too often, our machinations fail anyway. Others see our meanness for what it is, and we lose out on opportunities we might otherwise have had.

Helping someone else rise might well help me rise, too.

Silence and strength

"May the stars carry your sadness away,
May the flowers fill your heart with beauty.
May hope forever wipe away your tears,
And, above all, may silence make you strong."
CHIEF DAN GEORGE

Often, our first instinct when we're feeling sad is to fill up the empty space around us with people, noise, and activity. "Get out and see other people," our friends tell us. "Keep busy."

But it can be very healing to allow ourselves to feel our sadness fully, in silence and alone, particularly if we look for our solace in nature. Being in the natural world reminds us that everything, including sadness, eventually passes.

When I am sad, I will sit quietly and experience my feelings. By letting myself be sad for a while, I prepare myself to move beyond sadness.

Enthusiasm

"None are so old as those who have outlived enthusiasm."

HENRY DAVID THOREAU

Wrinkles, gray hair, and aches and pains aren't the real indicators of old age; a loss of interest in life is. If we are engaged in life, we're still young no matter what our chronological age. And if we have no enthusiasm for life, we can be old at any age.

We admire the eighty-year-old who is learning to surf, the sixty-year-old who is going back to school, the seventy-year-old who joins the Peace Corps. Their willingness to try new things, to meet each new day with curiosity and excitement, is an example for us all, whatever our age.

I will approach this day with enthusiasm.

Excellence

> "*The secret of joy in work is contained in one word—excellence. To know how to do something well is to enjoy it.*"
>
> ～PEARL S. BUCK ～

*I*t doesn't matter what the work is—cleaning windows, delivering the mail, or designing rockets. We can find joy in any kind of work if we focus on the quality of our work. On the other hand, we're not likely to find joy in work that we do sloppily or ineptly.

We may not be excellent at everything we do, but we should always strive for excellence. And when we do, we may surprise ourselves at how much enjoyment we can take in even the most mundane tasks.

I do many things well, some of them more significant than others. But I can enjoy any task if I focus on doing it well.

Finding God

"The search for God is like riding around on an ox hunting for the ox."

We look far and wide for the answers to life's big questions when they may be much closer to us than we realize. How can we open our eyes to the ox we're riding on?

Today I will think about what is important in my life. But first I will put on my philosophical reading glasses so that I can see what is right before my eyes.

Finding inspiration

> ❝*You can't wait for inspiration. You have to go after it with a club.*❞
>
> ❧JACK LONDON☙

Some artists wait to be struck, like lightning, by inspiration and then follow the inspiration wherever it leads.

Others simply get up every day and go to work. They write until they've produced a certain number of words. Or they draw until they've completed a certain number of sketches. These artists don't wait for inspiration, they work. And work. And work. And eventually, inspiration makes an appearance.

I sometimes use lack of inspiration as an excuse for not doing things I say I love. Today I'm going to go ahead and do what I love and not wait to be inspired. If I have to, I'll make my own inspiration.

Growing with experience

"People grow through experience if they meet life honestly and courageously."
ELEANOR ROOSEVELT

If experience is such a great teacher, why are there so many people who have been through interesting or difficult experiences who don't seem to have learned much from them?

It's not the experience alone; it's the way we decide to deal with the experience. One person who loses a job may become depressed, withdraw, and blame others for his or her problems. Another may elect to go back to school, change careers, or relocate to a more prosperous area. Same experience, different results.

I have had—and will continue to have—difficult experiences. It's up to me to learn from them.

Trying to please

> "A 'no' uttered from deepest conviction is better and greater than a 'yes' merely uttered to please, or what is worse, to avoid trouble."
> — MAHATMA GANDHI

From the time we are little children, we are taught to please others. It's a hard habit to break, even when we know we are sacrificing honesty and sometimes integrity by trying to get along.

So we say yes, or we say nothing, when an unfair situation arises, because we don't want to "rock the boat"—we don't want people to think that we're hard to get along with. After we've said yes or nothing too many times, we lose sight of our own values.

I won't be mean or offensive, but if I don't say no when I see things that are wrong, who will? I'm strong enough to face the consequences if I "rock the boat."

An educated mind

"It is the mark of an educated mind to be able to entertain a thought without accepting it."

❧ ARISTOTLE ❧

Can we really be corrupted by hearing something we disagree with? We often act as if this were the case. We choose friends who tend to agree with us. We join organizations that believe what we believe. We live in places where everyone looks and acts pretty much like us.

How fragile must our beliefs be if we resist even listening to opposing ideas. How weak would we have to be to fear being susceptible to every idea that enters our mind.

The next time I'm ready to dismiss another person's ideas out of hand, I will stop myself and at least listen to what the person has to say. I still may dismiss the person's ideas, but I'll know something more about them—and my own.

Corny but true

"*There's an element of truth in every idea that
lasts long enough to be called corny.*"

IRVING BERLIN

*T*he younger we are, the more likely we are to
dismiss the past as being old-fashioned and
irrelevant. The older we are, the more likely we
are to see wisdom and virtue in "the good old
days."

We can't always predict, in our youth, which
ideas will prove to have the most-lasting merit.
On the other hand, as the years pass, we may
begin to overvalue some ideas simply because
they remind us of when we were younger. The
challenge is not reject ideas simply because they
seem corny or to embrace ideas simply because
they are nostalgic.

Which ideas from my youth are still good today?
And which should I let go of?

Hitting the target

"I never hit a shot, not even in practice, without having a very sharp, in-focus picture of it in my head."

JACK NICKLAUS

Imagine preparing to hit a golf ball with no idea of where we want it to go or how hard we need to hit it. Even the best golfers would fail miserably with such a handicap. In fact, the best golfers prepare to hit a golf ball by doing just the opposite: making the shot in their mind first. They see their shot and feel it in their bodies before they ever even hit the ball. Having the image in their head allows their body to do what is needed to make the image real.

I will visualize myself succeeding at one of my goals. How does it feel, in every part of my body? What do I see as I work towards success? Holding this image in my mind will help me achieve my goal.

Shared suffering

"When a good man is hurt, all who would be good must suffer with him."

❧ EURIPEDES ☙

Goodness does not exist in isolation. Every act of goodness contributes to the greater good. Similarly, when any act of goodness is delayed or thwarted, we all suffer.

Sometimes we see or hear about bad things being done to good people, and we don't do anything because the events seem so far away or disconnected from us. But when a good person is attacked, injured, arrested, jailed, tortured, or killed anywhere in the world, we are all diminished—and we are all a little less safe.

What can I do to support good people doing good things wherever they are? Can I send money? Join an organization? Write a letter of support? Contact a government official?

New worlds

"Each friend represents a world in us, a world possibly not born until they arrive."
    ❧ANAÏS NIN☙

Our friends are not all the same, and hooray for that. One friend brings out our athletic side; we run or go to the gym together. Another sharpens our intellect with debate and discussion. Yet another is our favorite companion for going to the movies or out to dinner.

Our friends are both like us and not like us, and it is the ways they are not like us that stimulates and awakens new possibilities in ourselves.

I am lucky to have friends who help me be a more interesting and active person than I would be without them.

New beginnings

"We see the brightness of a new page where everything yet can happen."

◆ RAINER MARIA RILKE ◆

One of the most wonderful things about being young is the sense that we still have the whole world in front of us. We haven't yet fixed our path one way or the other, and the horizon seems to extend endlessly before us. It's an exciting time.

Every choice we make in life closes off one or more possibilities. But choices can also open up possibilities. No matter what age we are, we can always look forward and imagine new paths that we might take.

No matter how old I am, there are always opportunities, always new things I can do.

Ideals

> "*Ideals are like the stars; we never reach them,*
> *but like the mariners of the sea, we chart our*
> *course by them.*"
>
> ❧CARL SCHURZ❧

We shouldn't become frustrated because we are never quite as good as we'd like to be—or that the world never lives up to our expectations. We will never reach all of our ideals. But we still need to have ideals and to make working towards them our life's mission. Without ideals, we would have nothing to strive for.

I may never be as good as I would like to be, but I will always strive to get closer to my ideal self.

Jealousy

"Jealousy is the only vice that gives no pleasure."
❧ ANONYMOUS ❧

We can be touched by jealousy, even when we know it's silly. Our kindergartner tells us she loves her teacher, and we're jealous. Our father praises one of our siblings, and we're jealous. Our partner remarks that a celebrity is attractive, and we're jealous.

Jealousy is not an indication of the strength of our feelings for the other person; it is an indication of our insecurity. If we're confident that our children, parents, and partner love us, we won't be jealous of their attention to others.

I have feelings of jealousy from time to time, but I don't need to make others suffer for it. I know who loves me, and I need to trust in this love.

Compassion

"*If you want others to be happy, practice compassion. If you want to be happy, practice compassion.*"

❧THE 14TH DALAI LAMA❧

Compassion is not the same thing as sympathy or pity. Compassion is a more powerful—and more difficult—emotion. Compassion means understanding the suffering of others—and wanting to do something about it.

Practicing compassion goes beyond merely shaking our heads and sighing, "Oh, that's too bad." We must first want to change the circumstances of others. And then we must try our best to change these circumstances.

It's easy for me to feel sorry for others. To be compassionate, though, I need to understand why people are suffering and then try to do something about it.

Helping words

"A helping word to one in trouble is often like a
switch in a railroad track . . . an inch between a
wreck and smooth, rolling prosperity."
HENRY WARD BEECHER

When friends or family members are troubled,
we wonder what we can say to them that will
really matter. In times of great sorrow or
distress, even the kindest words can seem trite
or ineffectual.

Often, though, it's not what we say that
matters, but that we care enough to say something. The words don't matter so much as the
thoughts and feelings behind them. And we
should never underestimate how much
sympathetic thoughts and feelings mean to
those in trouble.

It's important for me to show, with words and
deeds, that I care when someone close to me
needs help.

Thanks

"No duty is more urgent than that of returning thanks."

❧JAMES ALLEN❧

We take for granted that others know how grateful we are for their kindness and thoughtfulness towards us. We don't really need to send a card or make a phone call, do we?

But think how touched we are when someone sends us a special thank-you. Thanking others is not merely a social formality. It is an act of kindness and thoughtfulness in its own right.

If someone is kind to me, I can certainly take the time to write a thank-you note or to call them.

Seeking and striving

> **"**I am seeking.
> I am striving.
> I am in it with all my heart.**"**
> ❧VINCENT VAN GOGH❧

Greatness springs from deep commitment. Yet, as much as we may want to commit to greatness, our lives don't always seem to cooperate. We still have to get up every day and make breakfast, go to work, run errands, clean the house—all the quotidian activities that take up so much of our time.

The solution is a simple one: commit fully to even the most mundane tasks. We can live our life, every part of it, in every moment, with all our heart. The alternative is to live much of our life without passion.

I will consider each day a gift to be embraced with everything I have.

The benefit of tears

"A good cry lightens the heart."
YIDDISH PROVERB

We've known for a long time that a good cry can make us feel better. Scientists confirmed it years ago. Tears help us get rid of hormones that make us sad. Physiology aside, though, sometimes it just seems like we need to cry. It's part of a process of feeling sad and then getting past it.

We don't need to be embarrassed by our tears. They come for a reason, and we need to let them flow.

I need to cry sometimes. When I do, I'll let the tears come.

Seeking goals

> "*If a man does not know what port he is steering for, no wind is favorable to him.*"
>
> ❧ SENECA ☙

It's surprising how easy it can be to just let life send us careening this way and that, as if our boat has lost its rudder. We complain every step of the way, of course, about how bad our luck is, how nothing is turning out the way we want.

How can we be disappointed about where we land when we didn't know where we were going in the first place?

If I want my life to make sense, I need to start with a mental map of what direction I want to go.

The gift of friendship

"A friend is a gift you give yourself."
ROBERT LOUIS STEVENSON

Friends give us their friendship and all that goes with it: laughter, support, loyalty, trust, companionship, sympathy, new interests. When we give friendship, we get friendship in return. It truly is a gift we give ourselves.

Unfortunately, it's easy to become so busy, self-absorbed, or cautious that we shut ourselves off to the possibility of making new friends. Sometimes we even shut ourselves off to friends we already have. Opening ourselves to friendship takes time and commitment, and it involves some risk—but, oh, the possibilities!

I will try to be open to new friendships, maybe even unlikely friendships.

Perspective of age

"The man who views the world at fifty the same as he did at twenty has wasted thirty years of his life."

MUHAMMAD ALI

What adult over thirty doesn't like to be thought of as youthful? It flatters us when others assume that we're younger than we are.

Being young at heart, though, shouldn't mean being young at mind. If our perspective on the world doesn't widen and deepen as we age, then we're squandering the most valuable asset life has to offer.

I loved my younger years, but I also love how experience has informed my judgment and made me a wiser person.

The web of deception

66*Oh what a tangled web we weave,*
  *When first we practice to deceive.*99
  ❧ SIR WALTER SCOTT ❧

It starts with just a little fib: "Oh, we can't go to your party, sorry. Nothing serious, just a sore throat and a little fever, but we really don't want to spread any germs." Now we've got the evening to ourselves, and we didn't have to hurt anyone's feelings by saying no.

But then the fib grows. Our friends send over some chicken soup. We get a phone call asking if we're feeling better. Someone who went to the party runs into us the next week and expresses sympathy over our illness. It would have been a lot easier either to go to the party or to simply say that we preferred to stay home.

Even small lies get complicated quickly. I'm better off being as honest as I can be.

Seeing beauty

> *"I never saw an ugly thing in my life; for let the form of an object be what it may—light, shade, and perspective will always make it beautiful."*
> ~JOHN CONSTABLE~

Beauty—and ugliness—really are in the eye of the beholder. We can dismiss things in our lives as flawed and ugly. Or we can choose to see them in a different light that reveals their strengths and beauty.

If I'm tempted to dismiss something—or someone—as not worth my time, I will give it or them a second look, from a different perspective. I may have found someone uninteresting because I simply wasn't asking the right questions.

Preparedness

"In the field of observation, chance favors only the prepared mind."

🙚LOUIS PASTEUR🙚

Few people really "have all the luck." Most of those we envy have set the stage for their successes. They were ready for luck to come along because they'd studied or saved or watched for opportunities and then seized the moment.

We can prepare ourselves for luck as well. In fact, we'd better, or we may find ourselves out of luck in the long run.

I can't be lucky in life if I don't create circumstances that will allow me to prevail.

Finding fault

> *"To find a fault is easy; to do better may be difficult."*
>
> **PLUTARCH**

We all like to criticize, even if we have no idea how we would do any better than those we're criticizing. Sure, some people deserve to be criticized. But we could offer our criticism with a little humility, especially when we know that people are doing the best that they can and that we could probably not do any better ourselves.

I will try not to criticize someone unless I can offer a better solution.

What we eat

" Tell me what you eat, and I will tell you what you are. "

❧ ANTHELME BRILLAT-SAVARIN ✍

If we skip breakfast and grab fast food for lunch, what do we think of ourselves? If we eat a dinner of popcorn and soda while standing over the sink, what do we think of ourselves? If we repeatedly gorge ourselves on the comfort foods of our youth, what do we think of ourselves?

What and how we eat says a lot about us—and how we feel. We do not have to treat ourselves badly, eating food that neither nourishes nor delights us. We can change what and how we eat—and, in the process, what we think of ourselves.

I will respect myself—and take care of my body— by eating appropriately and enjoying what I eat.

Being ourselves

"The easiest thing in the world to be is you. The most difficult thing to be is what other people want you to be. Don't let them put you in that position."

❧ LEO BUSCAGLIA ☙

The urge to please is powerful, even when it pushes us to be someone we are not. When we try too hard to please, however, we usually fail to please anyone—not the person we were aiming to please and certainly not ourselves

If people can't accept us for who we are, then we have to ask ourselves why we would want to have a relationship with them to begin with. We should never have to be inauthentic to earn someone's love or respect.

I am who I am. While I can always improve, I will not let anyone try to make me what they want me to be.

Experience

> "*Experience is not what happens to a man; it is what a man does with what happens to him.*"
> **◆ ALDOUS HUXLEY ◆**

We all know people who have gone through experiences that should have made them stronger, more interesting, more confident, or more empathetic. Yet somehow they've passed through the experiences seemingly unphased.

We should see such people as cautionary examples of what happens when we fail to actively engage the world. Our experiences are not going to do anything for us unless we choose to do something with our experiences.

I will try to see every experience as a chance to learn about myself and grow into a better person.

Keeping quiet

"There's nothing wrong with having nothing to say—unless you insist on saying it."

ᚙANONYMOUSᚙ

The people we dread sitting next to at parties aren't the silent ones. However reticent the person next to us may be, we can usually find something to say. Or we can at least sit there in quiet companionship.

No, the people we dread are the ones who insist on filling every moment with the sound of their own voices. They babble on about everything while saying nothing, and we can't wait to find an excuse to get away from them.

I don't need to fill in every gap in every conversation. I can listen to others or just sit quietly. No one will think there's something wrong with me if I'm quiet—but they might if I insist on talking all the time.

Laughing together

> *"Laughter is the shortest distance between two people."*
>
> **VICTOR BORGE**

Make someone laugh, and we've made a friend. We're drawn to people who are amused by the same things that amuse us. It's a sign of other common interests and a similar outlook on life.

I enjoy laughing with new people. It helps me get to know them.

Freedom

> ❝*You can only protect your liberties in this world by protecting the other man's freedom. You can only be free if I am free.*❞
>
> ❧CLARENCE DARROW❧

Great societies are founded on the idea that everyone's freedom is important. Not freedom for the wealthy or freedom for the powerful, but freedom for everyone.

We don't always realize how we put our own freedoms at risk when we acquiesce to others losing theirs. "It won't happen to us," we say. "We're not doing anything wrong. We've got nothing to worry about." But history gives us many examples of freedoms lost, bit by bit, because people thought it couldn't happen to them.

I enjoy my freedom and know that it is something I need to protect. I will be as vigilant about protecting the freedoms of others as I am about my own.

The benefit of work

> "*Work banishes those three great evils:*
> *boredom, vice, and poverty.*"
>
> — VOLTAIRE —

Maybe the Puritans had it right: Work in and of itself is important. We're usually happiest when we're working—even as we're complaining that we need more time off!

Of course we can work too hard, and we're often tempted to do so. But working hard and staying busy puts food on the table, keeps us out of trouble, improves our outlook on life, and reminds us that we are useful and needed.

I complain about work, but I realize that I am lucky to have it.

Taking care of ourselves

"Call on God, but row away from the rocks."
INDIAN PROVERB

Having faith in the guidance of a higher power does not mean giving up responsibility for our own actions—or inactions. Whatever spiritual beliefs we may have, we know that life gives us opportunities to make choices. Recognizing these opportunities and acting accordingly is one of the ways that we honor our beliefs.

I pray for guidance when I am troubled, but I also need to take action to make things better. As the Bible says, God helps those who help themselves.

Being scared

> "*Being scared can keep a man from getting killed, and often makes a better fighter out of him.*"
> ❧LOUIS L'AMOUR☙

We don't need to be conquered by our fear. We can actually use it to help us to perform better. Few of us routinely engage in physical battles, but we all face battles of other sorts in the normal course of our lives. How do we confront the boss when an idea that management proposed isn't working? How do we give a presentation in front of a group when we're filled with stage fright?

Fear, if we let it, can paralyze us. Instead, why not use our fear to focus and motivate us? If we're afraid to confront the boss, use this fear to formulate a stronger case. If we're nervous about speaking in front of a group, use this fear to prepare a better presentation.

Instead of letting my fear overcome me, I'll use it to help me do better.

Getting too easily

"That which we obtain too easily, we esteem too lightly."

❧THOMAS PAINE☙

We value most the things we've worked hardest to get, whether it's a new car we've saved years to buy or the admiration of someone we know to be extremely demanding. "Yes," we say, "we did it. We've accomplished something."

This can be a good thing, because it encourages us to work hard. But we shouldn't forget to value those things we haven't had to work hard for: the love of a parent; the generosity of a friend; the beauty of a summer's day. Our challenge is to notice and esteem all the blessings we receive, whether we've "earned" them or not.

When I work for something, I know how valuable it is. I will try to appreciate the value of the gifts I receive as well.

Community

66 *There can be no vulnerability without risk; there can be no community without vulnerability; there can be no peace, and ultimately no life, without community.* 99

M. SCOTT PECK

Most of us are hesitant when we first join a new community. Will we fit in? Do we want to let the other members of the community into our lives? What does becoming a member of the community say about us? These are important questions to consider.

But we can't make the world a better place except by working with others. And we can't work with others if we merely stand in the background judging and withholding. We must be willing to risk vulnerability if we want to be an engaged member of a real community.

I am willing to risk being vulnerable because I believe in the power of community.

Asking for nothing

"We never reflect how pleasant it is to ask for nothing."

⬧ SENECA ⬧

It can be very unpleasant to ask others for the things we need. Often what we ask for is given freely and with love, but we are still uncomfortable asking for it. We tend to feel weak or inferior when we have to ask others for help.

What we rarely think about, though, is how pleasant it is not to have to ask for someone else's help. Not needing is a good feeling, but not needing to ask may be an even better feeling.

I will not be embarrassed about asking for help when I need it, but I will also appreciate the times when I don't have to ask for anything.

Room at the top

"There is always room at the top."
❧ DANIEL WEBSTER ❧

In a zero-sum game, no one can win without someone else suffering a corresponding loss.

Fortunately, life is not a zero-sum game, though there are some who seem to believe that it is. We don't have to push others aside to be winners. And we don't have to enjoy our successes alone.

In fact, sharing our successes with others can make them much more meaningful and pleasurable.

I want to succeed—and to include others with me as I do.

Summer's song

"In summer, the song sings itself."
— WILLIAM CARLOS WILLIAMS —

The sounds of birds chirping, insects humming, leaves rustling, rain falling, children playing, dogs barking . . . . We may be stuck inside during the winter months, but summer blurs the boundaries between inside and outside.

No matter where we live, summer is a special season. It's a time of richness, warmth, freedom, ease, and pleasure—a time when all of our senses are fully engaged.

I'm happy that it's summer. I want to drink in as much of it as I can.

Through the window

"Better keep yourself clean and bright; you are the window through which you must see the world."
GEORGE BERNARD SHAW

We perceive the world through the unique lens of our own beliefs and feelings. This is why we can see things so differently from our closest friend or the person who lives next door.

Our perspective can enhance our experience of the world—or distort it. To see the world clearly, we must continually examine and test our beliefs and assumptions so that we are not blinded by the fog of prejudice or the darkness of ignorance.

I want to see the world clearly. I will not let my vision be dulled by apathy, prejudice, or ignorance.

Bad luck

> *Those that are afraid of bad luck will never know good.*
>
> ⮞ RUSSIAN PROVERB ⮜

Life is a gamble. There's no way around it. We can't know good luck unless we're willing to risk having bad luck. And bad luck can come whether we take any risks or not. Clearly, we're better off taking an occasional risk—if we want to learn, grow, and become a better person.

I worry about what might happen to me, but I know I need to extend myself and take some chances if I am going to have a full life.

Opposition

"A certain amount of opposition is a great help to a man. Kites rise against, not with, the wind."
JOHN NEAL

We like it when other people agree with us. But we tend to make our biggest mistakes when no one offers any alternative ideas for what we're planning to do.

Even though we don't like it much when others question our ideas, it's often what prods us to look harder at those ideas, to refine and improve them.

I am glad that some people in my life are willing to argue with me, even when—or especially when—I'm convinced I know exactly what I'm doing.

Blindness

"One may have good eyes and yet see nothing."
❧ITALIAN PROVERB❧

Driving the same roads over and over, we stop noticing the people, homes, yards, and buildings along the way. We work with the same people for years but never see them as anything more than a reflection of the work they do. We've gotten so used to doing things a certain way, we can't see that there are better ways of doing these things—if we would just open our eyes.

To truly *see* what's around us, we have to make an effort. Life is too short to take the world for granted.

I will deliberately open my eyes to the world.

Trying again

"Big shots are only little shots who keep shooting."
❧ CHRISTOPHER MORLEY ❧

Few people simply leap to the top of their profession. Most get there incrementally—step by step, experience by experience, and even mistake by mistake.

If we give up, we fail for certain. To have even a chance at success, we have to keep reloading and taking aim at our target.

Instead of complaining about how frustrating my failures are and how others seem to have it so much better than me, I will just keep plugging along towards what I want.

Charm

> ❝*A beauty is a woman you notice; a charmer is one who notices you.*❞
>
> ❧ADLAI STEVENSON❧

We admire the life of the party, the person who attracts others with his or her wit and wisdom. We envy the "looker," the person who attracts others with his or her beauty and physical attributes.

But the people we really want to be around are the ones who show an interest in us. When they ask about our likes and dislikes, laugh at our jokes, compliment our appearance, we feel good about them—and ourselves.

I won't worry about whether I'm having a good time at an event. I'll see what I can do to help others enjoy themselves.

A leap in the dark

> "*All growth is a leap in the dark, a spontaneous, unpremeditated act without benefit of experience.*"
> ❧HENRY MILLER❧

Our experience helps us make wiser choices, and making wiser choices allows us to take fewer risks.

But we stagnate unless we take an occasional leap in the dark—without planning for it, without analyzing it in advance. We don't know exactly where we're going to land. We just know we have to reach out, take a chance, and see what happens.

I'm generally cautious, and that's a good thing. But I recognize that sometimes I just have to go ahead and try something new. Even if things don't go well, I will have learned something important from taking the chance.

Desire

> **"***If men could regard the events of their own lives
> with more open minds, they would frequently
> discover that they did not really desire the things
> they failed to obtain.***"**
> — ANDRÉ MAUROIS

We desire things we think will make us happy.
Maybe it's something we want to own—a larger
house, for example. Or maybe it's something
we want to do—swim the English Channel. But
often, fulfilling our desires is less satisfying than
we'd imagined.

Why is this so? Some of the things we think
we want exist largely in our imagination. No
reality could ever compete with the fantasy
we've created about the objects of our desire.

I will not let my desire for things I don't have
keep me from appreciating those I do. There's a
good chance I don't really want some things as
much as I think I do.

Progress

> **"***Whenever you take a step forward, you are bound to disturb something.***"**
>
> ❧INDIRA GANDHI☙

The path of "true anything" isn't always smooth. Almost any aspect of our life can be disturbed as we pursue and accomplish goals that are important to us. Going to college may mean separating from parents. A promotion may mean a different relationship with coworkers. Marriage may mean losing—and gaining—friends.

The only way to prevent such disturbances would be to avoid ever taking a step forward. But who wants to stand in one place?

I recognize that each time I step forward, I may stir things up. I can't avoid these disturbances, but I can accept them and move on.

Taking time

"No great thing is created suddenly."

❧ EPICTETUS ❧

It takes time to build a relationship, a career, a house. If we try to speed the process up, we're likely to become frustrated. Worse, we may build something that is less than what we had hoped for.

As I put together the pieces of my life, I recognize that I cannot—and should not—hurry the important things. I want whatever I build to be sturdy and long-lasting.

Looking around

"Do not look back in anger, or forward in fear, but around in awareness."

JAMES THURBER

We look back in anger at the people who've hurt us, the frustrations we've felt, the bad luck we've endured. We look forward in fear at the possibility that we might lose our job, contract a disease, or suffer the death of a loved one.

The place we need to be is right here, right now—not looking anxiously at what has been or what might be, but fully aware of what is.

I take a deep breath, knowing that I'm lucky to be alive. I have survived challenges in the past and will survive challenges in the future. Nothing need distract me from living my life today.

Giving of ourselves

"*You give but little when you give of your possessions. It is when you give of yourself that you truly give.*"

— KAHLIL GIBRAN

When a charity asks for our help, it's easy to write a check. When a friend is ill, it's easy to send a card or gift.

But it would mean a lot more—to the charity and to our friend—if we gave of ourselves instead of our money. It would also mean a lot more to us. We waste so much time in meaningless activities: watching television, gossiping, fretting about things we can't change. If we could devote just part of this time to helping others, we'd all be better off.

I tell myself I'm too busy to volunteer or to volunteer more than I do. But if I look at my schedule carefully, I can find the time.

Speaking the truth

" Truth is always exciting. Speak it, then; life is dull without it. "

❧ PEARL S. BUCK ❧

In our attempts to be polite, we may stifle our best, most heartfelt ideas and beliefs. We're afraid we might hurt someone else's feelings if we spoke truthfully.

But it is possible to be honest without being rude or mean. How else do we let others know who we are? How can others let us know who they are? Unless we speak the truth, no bad idea will be challenged and no good idea will be shared.

Censoring my true thoughts cuts me off from others. I don't need to stifle my ideas. I can express my true self in ways that are not hurtful.

Being with children

" *The soul is healed by being with children.* **"**
🙥 FYODOR DOSTOYEVSKI 🙢

A good cure for being bored, frustrated, or depressed is to spend some time with children. Everything is new to them—and this fresh outlook can be catching. Walking with a child, we can see again, as if for the first time, the bright beauty of flowers, the relentless diligence of insects, the myriad shapes of clouds.

Children make us slow down, to match their gait. They ask questions—questions we may have forgotten we know the answers to. Their young eyes notice things we have not really looked at for years.

When I am with children—my own or someone else's—I'll pay attention to them and to what they bring into my life.

Field of vision

"Every man takes the limits of his own field of vision for the limits of the world."
          ❧ARTHUR SCHOPENHAUER❧

It's easy to assume that what we see and think represents the world at large. Our friends and family tend to share our outlook, and this reinforces our sense of the universality of our perspective. We get comfortable using such expressions as "Everyone knows . . ." or "We all believe . . ." without considering what a small sample "everyone" and "we" refers to.

Searching out friends and acquaintances of varied backgrounds and experiences, and learning about their perspectives, helps make us more aware of how limited our viewpoint is.

I have firmly held beliefs—and need to recognize that others may hold different beliefs just as firmly.

Good and bad habits

" *The unfortunate thing about this world is that the good habits are much easier to give up than the bad ones.* **"**

W. SOMERSET MAUGHAM

We vow to exercise every day—then the weather turns bad, we have conflicts in our schedule, and suddenly we don't feel up to it anymore. We vow to send thank-you notes for every gift we receive—but we get busy, time goes by, and then what's the point? We vow to eat healthier foods, but we're in a rush, a fast-food restaurant is close by, and there goes our diet.

Why is it so easy to stop doing things that are good for us, yet so hard to give up bad habits?

I will try to make my good habits stronger than my bad habits. I will list all my habits so that I can track how well I'm reinforcing the good ones and extinguishing the bad ones.

Waiting for success

> **"***I couldn't wait for success, so I went ahead
> without it.***"**
>
> ~JONATHAN WINTERS~

Too often we try to postpone our lives while
we wait to reach one goal or another. We put
off dating until we've lost a certain amount of
weight. We wait to have people over for dinner
until we can afford nicer furniture. We delay
having children until we're more successful in
our career.

But life doesn't wait. It just keeps going,
whether we're where we want to be or not.

I like the idea of throwing myself into life—
success or no success.

Small differences

"We must not, in trying to think about how we can make a big difference, ignore the small daily differences we can make which, over time, add up to big differences that we often cannot foresee."
MARIAN WRIGHT EDELMAN

There are so many problems in the world, how do we begin to make a dent in fixing them? It's so easy to become discouraged when we think about how much there is to do and how little there is to do it with.

But we can do something. If we can't afford to give $100 to a charity, $10 is better than nothing. If we can't volunteer our time every week, even a few hours a year helps. And if enough of us act this way, we can change the world.

Every day, I can do something to better the world, even if it's just offering a kind word to someone who needs it.

In the race

"*I've got something inside of me, peasantlike and stubborn, and I'm in it till the end of the race.*"
≈ TRUMAN CAPOTE ≈

We don't have to make elaborately detailed plans about how we're going to lead our lives (although it's good to do some planning along the way.) We can simply set a course and pledge to hang in there, whatever comes. This, in the end, is the most courageous and powerful thing we can say.

I am here and I'm staying. Whatever life throws at me, I will not be stopped.

Getting through

"The best way out is always through."
ROBERT FROST

There's no easy way to get out of a difficult period, as much as we may want to find one. We just have to go through it. Rationally, we may know that our pain will lessen over time, but this is little solace at first.

Still, we survive. And we survive by living through our pain—day by day, week by week, month by month. And then, suddenly one day, we're on the other side, looking back, thinking, "That was a rough period, wasn't it? But I made it."

I want things to be better—I want to be better—right away. I hate being in pain. But I can't make the healing go any faster, so I just need to accept that I will heal, with time.

Bringing peace

"First keep the peace within yourself, then you can also bring peace to others."

❧ THOMAS À KEMPIS ☙

We tell our friends to calm down, stop worrying, remember that life is good. But the admonitions don't mean much unless we can follow them ourselves.

Finding a way to be peaceful, to accept our worries and our problems without fretting, is a constant challenge for all of us. Peacefulness is contagious, though. Once we find it, it has a way of spreading on its own to others.

I can create a moment of peace for myself every day, just sitting quietly and letting myself relax.

Ingenuity

> "*Never tell people how to do things. Tell them what to do and they will surprise you with their ingenuity.*"
>
> ❧GENERAL GEORGE S. PATTON☙

We have expectations about how things are supposed to be done, and we want others to meet those expectations. Dishes should be stacked just so. Dust first, then vacuum (or is it the other way around?). No, don't take that road, it's too slow.

When we force our ideas onto others, though, we not only show that we don't respect them, we miss out on discovering new and interesting ways to accomplish things.

If I trust others to do things their way, I may find that their way is better than mine.

Boredom

> *"Boredom is the feeling that everything is a waste of time; serenity, that nothing is."*
>
> ❖THOMAS SZASZ❖

It's all a matter of attitude: A day with nothing to do stretches in front of us. We get antsy, aimlessly wandering around the house, watching television, or flipping through magazines. We heave a few big sighs, wonder what our friends are doing, and begin to beat ourselves up for being so lazy. Can't wait for the day to end.

Or we can see the day as a gift. No responsibilities, no plans. We can savor the morning cup of coffee, take a long walk with no destination in mind, listen to our favorite piece of music, write an entry in our journal—all of the things we say we're too busy to do most of the time.

I don't need to be busy to avoid being bored. I will let myself enjoy just being.

The potential of miracles

"I'm in love with the potential of miracles.
For me, the safest place is out on a limb."
SHIRLEY MACLAINE

Miracles happen more often than we think, but we have to be open to their possibilities to experience them. Accepting the possibilities of miracles involves taking some risks. We can't find our true calling if we don't risk being rejected. We can't fall in love if we're not willing to risk being hurt. We can't make a difference in the lives of others if we're afraid to take a chance or make a sacrifice.

I'll keep my eyes open for any miracles that may come my way, if I let them.

Laughing with friends

"That is the best—to laugh with someone because you think the same things are funny."
    ❧ GLORIA VANDERBILT ❧

Friendships often are forged by laughter. Someone with the same sense of humor is likely to have other similarities we value.

We look forward to getting together with long-time friends to enjoy a great roar of laughter. We know each other well enough, have spent enough time together, to understand each other's sense of humor. The funniest stories we share are those about ourselves and the things we've done together.

I will laugh today with people I love.

Self-disclosure

"If you do not tell the truth about yourself,
you cannot tell it about other people."
❧ VIRGINIA WOOLF ❧

When we recognize our own flaws—and our own strengths—and can share them with others, we have more credibility when we assess the flaws and strengths of those around us. In fact, we have more credibility in all that we do when we are honest about ourselves with others.

I know what I do well and what I don't do well. I know the mistakes I've made in the past and the successes I've had. I don't need to paint a false picture to others. I can tell my story just as it is.

Love within reach

"*When we cannot get what we love, we must love what is within our reach.*"

FRENCH PROVERB

Learning to love what we have, rather than what we would like to have, is not a matter of giving up or compromising. It's a matter of maturing.

We set our goals high, and we should. We work diligently towards our goals, and we should. But if we don't realize all of our goals, should we live our lives with bitterness and regret? How much richer would our lives be if we could appreciate the blessings that we already have?

I will love my life for what it is rather than regretting it for what it is not.

Sins

"All sins are attempts to fill voids."
❧ SIMONE WEIL ❧

We all have bad habits. Smoking, drinking, gambling. Or, more mundanely, watching too much television, gossiping about others, eating too many sweets.

Why do we do these things? Because we're bored, stressed out, unhappy, sad, frustrated, lonely. We do them to feel better, but, too often, they only make us feel worse. We'll never be able to stop these bad habits until we understand the reasons behind them and address those reasons directly.

Instead of being hard on myself because of the unhealthy things I do, I will focus on the reasons I feel I need my bad habits.

Respecting others

"*It is terrible to destroy a person's picture of himself in the interests of truth or some other abstraction.*"

DORIS LESSING

Isn't the truth always best? When we're talking about ourselves, it is. But we don't need to hurt others in our desire to be truthful.

Maybe we're annoyed that our neighbor poses as an intellectual when he clearly isn't. Maybe we giggle when we see a woman who wants to be considered attractive but is dressed inappropriately. Maybe we know that an achievement a child is proud of means little. But we do no good by telling the truth in these circumstances. And we may do great harm.

Even when I'm short-tempered, I will respect others' self-esteem. I can argue without trying to destroy the self-image of those I argue with.

Tomorrow's joke

" *The crisis of today is the joke of tomorrow.* "
～ H.G. WELLS ～

When we're in the midst of a dreadful time, it often helps to remember that one day we'll be able to tell a great story about it, one we'll laugh at. We'll laugh because, in retrospect, what we thought was a crisis really wasn't so serious after all. Or we'll laugh because we made it through the crisis and came out stronger on the other side.

I'll try to keep my perspective, remembering that even the worst day is only one small moment in my life.

Sense of wonder

> "*The possession of knowledge does not kill the sense of wonder and mystery. There is always more mystery.*"
>
> ❧ANAÏS NIN☙

The more we learn, the more we realize how amazing is the world we live in—and how little we know about it.

Some may worry that the marvelousness of the world will be diminished if they learn too much of the science that describes it. Will we still enjoy a bird's song if we know the physics and biology of its articulation or the mating ritual it expresses? Of course. If anything, we will enjoy it more.

I will take every opportunity I can to learn about this wonderful universe I am part of.

Criticism

"Don't find fault, find a remedy."
HENRY FORD

We spend a lot of time knocking others for what they have done wrong without offering much in the way of useful ideas ourselves.

Problems need solutions. We may not have the answer, but we can at least offer ideas and support to those trying to work through problems.

Before criticizing, I need to find a way to help solve a problem.

The story of love

> " *The story of a love is not important—what is important is that one is capable of love. It is perhaps the only glimpse we are permitted of eternity.* "
>
> HELEN HAYES

When we love someone, we can become our best selves. Of course we want to be loved in return, and we want our love to last.

But even when this doesn't happen, we know that we are better for having been able to love. And if we can love once, we can love again.

I am a person who can love. I grow each time I love.

Faith

" *What we need is not the will to believe, but the wish to find out.* "

 BERTRAND RUSSELL

Faith involves a leap of imagination. Real faith also involves a searching, a desire to find answers to life's most difficult questions. We may have faith that follows the teachings of an organized religion, or we may have faith we have acquired through our own experiences and study. In either case, we do not betray our faith when we continue to search for meaning. Rather, we deepen and strengthen it.

My faith sustains me—and leads me on a continuous search for more knowledge.

Irritation

"*Everything that irritates us about others can lead us to an understanding of ourselves.*"
— CARL GUSTAV JUNG

Certain people rub us the wrong way. We're not exactly sure what it is about them we don't like: the way they talk or look or act. But we do know we don't like them, and our reaction seems out of proportion to any particular offense.

If we look closer, we may find that the irritation has nothing to do with anything these people have done or not done. Rather, they may simply remind us of others from our past with whom we've had problems. Or maybe they remind us of something we don't like about ourselves. What we're reacting to is something in our own history or personality.

When I find myself reacting negatively to someone, I'll try to figure out if the irritation is really about me.

Adventure

"Make voyages! Attempt them! There's nothing else."

✒ TENNESSEE WILLIAMS ✒

Most of our life we're advised to live cautiously. To buckle our seat belts. To look both ways before crossing a street. To save money. To stay in school. To eat healthy foods. To get regular checkups. Avoiding foolish risks is, of course, good advice. Still, we can't grow unless we take some risks. Occasionally we need to take advantage of one of the adventures that life offers us.

I want to be able to look back and know that I didn't just plod through my life. I had an adventure.

Failures

> **"***I have not failed. I've just found 10,000 ways that won't work.***"**
>
> **🌿THOMAS EDISON🌿**

We should drop the word *failure* from our vocabulary. It's misleading to think about our efforts in a strictly binary way—as either successes or failures.

Life is not this simple. Do babies fail when they try to take their first step and fall? That first step (and the tumble to the ground that inevitably follows it) is an integral and unavoidable part of the process of learning.

I will reframe my failures as necessary steps on the path to learning and growth.

A great wind

> *"A great wind is blowing, and that gives you either imagination or a headache."*
>
> — CATHERINE THE GREAT

There are two ways we can approach times of turmoil and upheaval: as opportunities for new ideas and new actions or as excuses for withdrawing from life and avoiding risk.

People with creativity and imagination often thrive in times of great change. People who don't consider themselves creative or imaginative tend to be concerned only with hunkering down and protecting themselves.

I won't let troubled times get the best of me. I'll treat them as a challenge to come up with new ideas.

Laughter

❝*The most wasted of all days is one without laughter.***❞**

～E.E. CUMMINGS～

Luckily, laughter is easy to come by. It doesn't cost anything. It's available to everyone, regardless of race, creed, or religion. It's contagious and spreads easily. And if we can't find something to laugh at, we can always laugh at ourselves.

I'm ready to laugh right now.

Taking action

"All you have to do is look straight and see the road, and when you see it, don't sit looking at it —walk."

🔊 AYN RAND 🔊

We've done our research. We've talked with friends and family. We've made lists and created plans. Now we have to double-check everything so that we can be certain everything is right before we move ahead.

But sometimes we can plan ourselves right out of an opportunity by trying to make everything too perfect. Sooner or later, we have to stop planning and get moving.

It may be more important for me to take action than it is to make sure my plan is perfect.

Today

"Yesterday is ashes; tomorrow wood. Only today does the fire burn brightly."

ESKIMO PROVERB

We are here, right now, in the middle of today. We have many wonderful memories of the past, and we have hopes for what will happen in the future. But it's today we are living.

I will not let today slip by without living it as fully as I can.

Goals

> "*If you would hit the mark, you must aim
> a little above it.*"
> ❧HENRY WADSWORTH LONGFELLOW☙

There's no shame in not meeting all of our goals, as long as our goals make us stretch. If we want to run a marathon in under three hours, we'll train differently than if we want to run it in four hours. Maybe we won't finish in three hours, but we'll likely do better than if we were striving for four.

This doesn't mean we should set goals that are impossible. If we do, there's a good possibility that we'll become frustrated and quit.

I will set realistic goals that challenge me and try hard to meet them. Maybe, just maybe, I will achieve these goals. If I don't, I will still have done well.

Time out

"*Live with no time out.***"**
SIMONE DE BEAUVOIR

We can't push the "pause" button on our lives. Every day counts, whether we're doing our best or our worst.

But even if we could call a time out when life becomes tense and stressful, would we really want to? Our life's clock keeps ticking no matter what. The only thing we truly have is time. Better to live every moment than to lose that time forever.

As much as I may want to call a time out in my life, I will live every moment as fully as I can.

Being somebody

> **"***I always wondered why somebody doesn't do something about that. Then I realized I was somebody.***"**
>
> ❧ LILY TOMLIN ☙

How many times have we walked past a piece of litter on the ground, cursing whoever was so thoughtless as to drop it and wondering when someone would come by to clean it up?

It wouldn't be hard for us to bend over and pick up that litter, then drop it in the nearest waste bin. Often, though, we don't because we think it's someone else's responsibility. Maybe it is, in an official way, but if each of us picked up just one piece of litter, the streets would be clean in no time.

When I can, I won't wait for somebody else to be responsible for addressing a problem. I'll take responsibility myself.

Mistakes

“*Mistakes are part of the dues one pays for a full life.*”

ߊSOPHIA LORENߊ

We can't have an interesting life without making a few mistakes here and there. We hope they won't be dangerous mistakes or mistakes that hurt other people. But there will be mistakes.

We can see our mistakes as things we'd like to forget—or as our most interesting, challenging, and stimulating experiences. Not because of the mistakes themselves, but because of what we learned from them.

I'm going to make mistakes. I will forgive myself and learn from them.

Staying angry

> *"Holding on to anger is like grasping a hot coal with the intent of throwing it at someone else; you are the one who gets burned."*
>
> ❧BUDDHA☙

People who hold grudges, who never stop talking about those who have wronged them, let their anger rule their lives. Those they're angry at may not care or even be aware of the grudge.

"But our anger is justified," we argue. Maybe, but does this justify the self-damage inflicted by holding on to and nursing the hurt? How many times must we bore our friends with another recounting of the injustice we've suffered? How much longer must we let our anger sour our outlook on life?

It's normal to get angry sometimes. But I'll do whatever I need to do to let my anger go and move on with my life.

Opportunity for kindness

> *"You cannot do a kindness too soon, for you never know how soon it will be too late."*
> ➤ RALPH WALDO EMERSON ➤

We shouldn't wait for the perfect moment to give a compliment or do a favor. Moments come and go too quickly. If we wait for them, we're likely to miss them altogether.

We should always indulge an urge to do something nice for others. When the impulse hits, go with it. Give the compliment. Do the favor. Say something that will cheer a friend.

I don't want to miss the chance to be kind to those around me. So I won't.

Strength

"What does not destroy me, makes me stronger."
FRIEDRICH WILHELM NIETZSCHE

Tough times can make us stronger and wiser. Knowing this doesn't really make tough times any easier, though—at least not while we're going through them. But it's worthwhile to remind ourselves often of this truth.

Of course, we get stronger not simply because we go through tough times, but because we call upon our best selves to find our way through them. We draw on our humor, patience, courage, and other qualities and, in doing so, learn the power of our inner resources.

I will survive the difficult periods in my life. And after each one, I will be a stronger, more resilient person.

Time for change

"Change before you have to."

❧JACK WELCH❧

When we have to change, we change. When we have no other choice, we do what we have to do. We may not like it—we may even resent it—but we do it anyway, and we find a way to deal with it.

But what if instead of simply reacting to change, we initiated change ourselves? What if we anticipated the need for change and actively planned for it in both our personal and professional lives? What if we acted before change was forced on us?

If change is good—and it can be—maybe I should deliberately push myself to change once in a while.

Ego and position

"Avoid having your ego so close to your position that when your position falls, your ego goes with it."

❧ COLIN POWELL ☙

We're proud when we're successful at what we do. Executive, teacher, athlete, parent—we like telling people what we do. It tends to be how we define who we are—to ourselves and others.

But what happens when we retire or become empty-nesters? This can be a wrenching adjustment. We don't quite know how to introduce ourselves without a job attached to our name. Worse, we aren't even sure ourselves who we are. It's good to be invested in our work, as long as we remember that we aren't our work and our work isn't us. It's just something that we do.

I love my work, but my life—and who I am—are more than my work. I will make sure that I have other sources of satisfaction.

New possibilities

"What after all has maintained the human race on this old globe, despite all the calamities of nature and all the tragic failings of mankind, if not the faith in new possibilities and the courage to advocate them."

❧ JANE ADDAMS ❧

From the time Homo sapiens evolved, we have dreamed of a better world. Because of our dreams, we have left our homes on long, arduous, uncertain journeys over land and water. Because of our dreams, we have sent explorers into the deepest oceans and the far reaches of outer space.

Because of our dreams, we get up every morning with an enduring faith in the possibilities that this day may bring.

Typhoons, earthquakes, war, famine—you'd think the human race would have given up by now. But we keep on. My problems are tiny compared to what others have faced. I will keep on, no matter what is thrown my way.

The miracle of the world

" *This world, after all our science and sciences, is still a miracle: wonderful, inscrutable, magical and more, to whosoever will think it.* "
THOMAS CARLYLE

We have learned a lot about the world we live in, from the geology of the land beneath us, to the biology of the life that surrounds us, to the physics of the sky above us. We know how diamonds are formed, how waterfalls were created, how birds are able to migrate for thousands of miles, and much more.

Knowing these things, however, doesn't necessarily explain the world to us. We can understand the *how*, but we still don't know the *why*. Searching for the why is the occupation of a lifetime.

I am awed by the world I live in, and the more I know about it, the greater my sense of wonder about it.

The rat race

"The problem with winning the rat race is you're still a rat."

🙚 LILY TOMLIN 🙘

None of us likes to lose; we all want to be winners. But what, exactly, does winning mean? And what if we decide that we don't want to compete? Does this automatically make us a loser?

Maybe it's time to get rid of the idea that life is a kind of race. What if, instead, we saw life as a kind of dance, where the idea isn't to win but to learn new moves, execute them gracefully, and, above all, enjoy ourselves?

I want to win as much as the next person, but I don't feel obliged to accept someone else's definition of winning. My own definition of winning is to maintain my integrity, optimism, and compassion in the face of events that threaten these qualities.

Continuity

"Even if I knew that tomorrow the world would go to pieces, I would still plant my apple tree."

❧ MARTIN LUTHER ❧

To quietly and peacefully go about our business sometimes requires great courage. Events in the world or in our own lives may make us want to scream and wail, tear our hair out, or beat our heads against a wall. But we don't do any of those things. We square our shoulders, look straight ahead, and carry out our daily routines. We try to restore normality to what feels like chaos.

I admire people who just keep going, without bragging or feeling the need to tell everyone about it. I can be one of those people.

Beating the competition

> *"Don't bother just to be better than your contemporaries or predecessors. Try to be better than yourself."*
> **WILLIAM FAULKNER**

Sports has given us the concept of "personal best," the idea that our most important competition is with ourselves. Can we do better today than we did yesterday? Can we do even better tomorrow?

Competing with ourselves is healthier than competing with others. For one thing, there's no way to cheat. For another, there can be no envy or resentment—no "sore losing"—if we're competing against ourselves.

What do I want to improve on? I'll keep track of my personal bests so that I can continually try to "be better than myself."

Bad memory

"Happiness is good health and a bad memory."
🙟 INGRID BERGMAN 🙝

We worry a lot about forgetting things. We make notes and tuck them in our pockets or post lists in prominent places around the house. We keep our address book or daily calendar with us at all times. We practice little tricks for remembering names and places.

We would be happier, though, if we could forget some things. Let's forget about those occasions when people betrayed us, made us cry, or sinned against us. Let's forget about those times when we embarrassed ourselves, acted meanly, or let ourselves down. There's no point in wallowing in such memories—and plenty of reasons to move on.

My good memories I'll keep for a long time. My bad ones I'll let go.

Enjoying the detour

> *" The really happy person is the one who can enjoy the scenery on a detour. "*
>
> **❧ ANONYMOUS ❧**

Oops, we've run into a detour on our way to where we had planned to go. We thought we were going to law school or culinary school or on a trip to Europe, but something happened, and now we find ourselves working and living in places we never dreamed of.

Maybe someone close to us needed our help. Maybe our finances didn't work out the way we'd hoped. Maybe we unexpectedly fell in love. We can sigh over the plans that went awry—or we can be pleased about landing right where we are. Maybe we'll get back to those original plans, maybe not. Whatever we do, we're going to be happy.

I won't cry over what seem to be missed opportunities. I'll value the opportunities I have instead.

Going home

> "*There is nothing like returning to a place that remains unchanged to find the ways in which you yourself have altered.*"
>
> NELSON MANDELA

We love—or fear—our high school reunion because we don't quite know what we're going to find out about ourselves. How will people remember us? And how will this compare with who we are today?

We're likely to be both a little disappointed— maybe we haven't changed as much as we thought—and a little delighted. For a moment, we see ourselves through the eyes of people who knew us when we were younger.

I wonder what my former classmates would think of me now. How would I measure up against their expectations? Against my own?

Failing better

*"Ever tried. Ever failed. No matter. Try again.
Fail again. Fail better."*

❧ SAMUEL BECKETT ❧

We will fail, more often than we care to think.
We can learn from our failures . . . and we're
still going to fail in the future. The key is to fail
in new ways, not to keep repeating the failures
we've already experienced.

I won't get discouraged by failure, but I will try to
make sure that when I fail, it's because of something new, not because I'm stuck in a rut.

A world perspective

"*Our loyalties must transcend our race, our tribe, our class, and our nation; and this means we must develop a world perspective.*"

❧ MARTIN LUTHER KING, JR. ☙

Human beings have lived in groups since they first walked the earth. We identify with those closest to us, starting at home and spreading out to our neighborhood, school, city, state, and nation.

The pride we take, and the loyalty we feel, as a member of a group helps us feel protected and connected. But we must always remember that we are also members of a much larger group: humanity.

I'm proud of my ethnic background, religious affiliation, and nationality. These are all part of my identity. But I know that I am also part of a large and complex world where, to some degree, every person is a part of my "tribe."

Doing something

> "*In any moment of decision, the best thing you can do is the right thing, the next best thing is the wrong thing, and the worst thing you can do is nothing.*"
>
> **THEODORE ROOSEVELT**

What if we're wrong? What if we pick the wrong person to love, or the wrong job to devote ourselves to, or the wrong city to live in? We waffle and weave. Maybe we can put off the decision for a while. Maybe things will be clearer tomorrow.

Not making a decision is making a decision—and it may well be the worst decision we could make.

I'll do my research, talk to people I trust, and think hard. Then I'll make a decision and move forward. If it turns out that I've taken a wrong path, I can always turn around and go the right way. If I don't make a decision, I'll never know the right way to go.

What we are

"To become different from what we are, we must have some awareness of what we are."

▰ ERIC HOFFER ▰

We don't set out to lose weight without first knowing what we weigh to begin with. We can't know that we want to make a change until we first know we have a problem. Even when we've identified a problem, we need to know where we're starting from to understand the job ahead of us.

To make any change in our lives, we need to know where we are right now.

I will do my best to understand who I am so that I can understand how to be better than I am.

Consistency

"Consistency is the last refuge of the unimaginative."
❧OSCAR WILDE☙

"But we've always done it this way," we complain when someone challenges us to make a change. But sometimes it's good to change, even if just for the sake of change. Trying new things helps us become more flexible and open-minded—good traits to have when change is unavoidable.

If a particular change doesn't work out, we'll still have learned something that we can use in the future.

I am open to change. I will make a small change in my everyday routine, just to see how it feels.

Goodness

"Goodness is easier to recognize than to define."
❧ W. H. AUDEN ☙

We know people who appear to fit standard definitions of the word *good*, and yet we don't really like them all that much. We also know people who don't exhibit conventional notions of goodness, but we sense their warmth and generosity from the moment we meet them. We know that they are truly good.

Goodness is an inner quality we sense in others—and want to have in ourselves.

I try to be good, to myself and to others. I take as my models people I sense to be truly good.

Mental attitude

"Nothing can stop the man with the right mental attitude from achieving his goal; nothing on earth can help the man with the wrong mental attitude."

🞿 THOMAS JEFFERSON 🞿

"Can't do it." "Never could do it." "Never will be able to do it." "No one could do it." "We don't have the right resources." "We haven't been trained." "We don't have the time."

We're full of excuses for why we can't do something, even before we've made one small effort to get it done. Will we succeed? Not with this attitude. But if we take on the challenge with enthusiasm and energy, assuming that we're going to do just fine, we just might.

I may not be able to change the tasks that need to get done, but I can change my approach to them.

Love and work

"*Love and work are the cornerstones of our humanness.*"

≈ SIGMUND FREUD ≈

It's pretty simple: We need someone to love and we need something to do. We don't have to have romantic love. The someone we love can be a child, a friend, a parent, or even a pet. The something we do can be any kind of task or activity; it doesn't have to be a career.

When we love, we are our best selves. When we work, we feel needed, purposeful, complete. Together, these two things are the building blocks of a happy life. They are what makes us human.

If I don't have love in my life, I need to make room for it. If I don't have work, I need to find it. I understand that these two things are essential to my happiness.

New endings

"*Though no one can go back and make a brand new start, anyone can start from now and make a brand new ending.*"

❧ CARL BARD ☙

We can spend a lot of time analyzing the bad decisions we've made, the mistakes we've made, the friends we've hurt. If only we'd been smarter, more patient, or just nicer. We can't change the past, no matter how much we analyze it.

But we can move forward in new ways, making better decisions, avoiding the old mistakes, and being nicer to those around us. We have countless opportunities to reinvent or reorient ourselves.

I don't have to be defined by things I've done in the past. I can make the future what I want it to be.

Learning from mistakes

66 *To make no mistake is not in the power of man;*
but from their errors and mistakes the wise and
good learn wisdom for the future. 99

PLUTARCH

Our resume doesn't show the mistakes we've made, which is unfortunate, because our mistakes tell a story of their own. Not of failure, but of opportunities for growth and change. It's not that we've made mistakes that matters, but how we've learned from our mistakes.

I hate making mistakes, but I know they're inevitable. Instead of beating myself up over them, I'll use them as learning experiences.

Compliments

"I can live for two months on a good compliment."
MARK TWAIN

We might not think a casual compliment means all that much, but consider how we feel after someone tells us we've done a good job, we look good today, or they admire one of our many fine qualities. We hold our head a little higher, smile a little more broadly, step a little more brightly.

When someone gives us a compliment, we tend to think better of them, too. Clearly, they're smart and insightful.

I enjoy it when someone gives me a compliment, and why not? It prompts me to give compliments as well.

Being gifted

> **"***It is one thing to be gifted and quite another thing to be worthy of one's own gift.***"**
>
> **❧NADIA BOULANGER❧**

Extraordinary talent doesn't, unfortunately, mean extraordinary character. If we're fortunate enough to stand out in some way, we should acknowledge this as a gift, not an entitlement.

I may be able to do something better than most others, and I'm fortunate if that's the case. But I am not a better person than others simply because of my talent.

Changing seasons

"To be interested in the changing seasons is a happier state of mind than to be hopelessly in love with spring."

GEORGE SANTAYANA

Cold weather helps us appreciate warm weather more—and warm weather helps us appreciate cold weather. With a change in seasons, there are so many things to anticipate. During the course of a year we watch trees change from bare to green to orange and red and gold to brown and back to bare again. Then there's the miracle of budding and greening all over again the next year.

As I enjoy the change of seasons, I can enjoy the changes in my life.

Middle of the road

“*We know what happens to people who stay in the
middle of the road. They get run over.*”
> ❧AMBROSE BIERCE❧

If one person we care about believes passionately
in one side of an issue and another believes
passionately in the other side, is it our role to be
somewhere in the middle—somewhere we think
we won't upset anyone?

There are times when the middle of the road
looks as good as anyplace else to stand, but
often we have strong feelings, too. It's okay to
express our beliefs, even if this might upset
someone we care about. If we don't take a stand,
we risk upsetting everyone.

I don't want to play it safe all the time. Playing it
safe can be riskier than following my feelings.

Limits of reality

" *The problems of the world cannot possibly be
solved by skeptics or cynics whose horizons are
limited by the obvious realities. We need men who
can dream of things that never were.* "
JOHN F. KENNEDY

If solving problems just meant doing the same
things we always do, we'd all be problem-free.
To solve problems—in our personal lives or in
the world—we sometimes need wild creativity;
we need ideas that seem crazy at first.

Some of those wild ideas won't work. Maybe
most of them won't work. But any problem only
needs one solution.

How can I get myself out of a rut when I'm trying
to deal with a problem? I'll stop censoring myself
and look beyond the horizon of obvious realities.

Recovering

"Suffering isn't ennobling, recovery is."
— CHRISTIAAN BARNARD —

We've all heard that suffering makes us stronger, that we learn from our difficulties. This may be true, but not in the simple way we might think. Difficult times don't make us better; *working through difficult times* does. Suffering can force us to draw on strengths we never knew we had. Discovering these hidden strengths can then help us cope should difficult times come again.

I hate bad times as much as anyone does, but I know I'm strong enough to get through them and recover from them.

Knowledge vs. wisdom

"Knowledge can be communicated but not wisdom."

—HERMANN HESSE—

Knowing things is not the same as being wise. Knowledge is the accumulation of facts and information; wisdom is knowledge tempered by experience and perspective. We can acquire knowledge from others. Becoming wise is a journey that we each must travel on our own.

I want to learn as much as I can, from every possible source. This will help me be smarter and more knowledgeable. But however knowledgeable I may become, there is no shortcut to becoming wise. I have to live and experience success and failure, day by day.

Depending on ourselves

> "*Faced with crisis, the man of character falls back on himself. He imposes his own stamp of action, takes responsibility for it, makes it his own.*"
> ❧CHARLES DE GAULLE❧

Ultimately, we're responsible for what we choose to do or not do. If we're lucky, we have great support from friends and family, but at some point we have to make decisions and take responsibility for them. Right or wrong, it's up to us. We take a deep breath, consider the advice we've been given, draw on our experience . . . and do what we think is best. If things work out, we are relieved. If they don't, we accept responsibility and move on.

I get lots of advice and support, but I recognize that in the end, it's up to me to make the major decisions in my life.

Helping

>❝*When a friend is in trouble, don't annoy him by asking if there is anything you can do. Think up something appropriate and do it.*❞
>
> ❧E. W. HOWE❧

"Let me know if there's anything I can do to help" may be one of the most useless thing we can say. People overwhelmed by illness, grief, or hardship can't or won't always ask for the help they need. Even if they can identify and express what they need, they may feel reluctant to ask.

Are there dishes to be washed? Children to be watched? Lawns to be mowed? The simplest tasks of ordinary life may be going undone during a crisis. Pick up a dish towel or grab a lawn mower, and just do what needs to be done.

I will help others in need by taking on some of the mundane—but essential—activities they are too distracted to handle.

Breaking someone's spirit

> "*It is easy—terribly easy—to shake a man's faith in himself. To take advantage of that, to break a man's spirit, is devil's work.*"
> —GEORGE BERNARD SHAW

Our words are such powerful weapons—more painful, in their way, than clubs or bullets. A few ugly words, and we can make others cry in sadness or anger. Constant criticism can make anyone feel inadequate and small.

No good comes of making others feel small. Any satisfaction we might momentarily feel from flinging ugly words fades quickly, and the pain of these words eventually comes back on us one way or another.

I don't want to hurt anyone with my words, even when I'm angry.

Love in our heart

"If you find it in your heart to care for somebody else, you will have succeeded."
>MAYA ANGELOU

It's easy to fall in love, harder simply to love. When we fall in love, we desire love in return. When we simply love, we give ourselves freely. We become our best selves when we love in this way.

While there is much we might hope to accomplish in our lifetime, to love, and love well, should top the list.

I want not only to be in love, but to love.

Changing perspective

"*A weed is no more than a flower in disguise.*"
❧JAMES LOWELL❧

What makes a weed different from a flower, except the way we view it? A dandelion shows us a sunny yellow flower in no way inferior to a daisy or a zinnia. Then the flower magically becomes a fluffy white ball, disappearing with the gentlest breeze. Can a zinnia do that?

All of us have weeds in our life—difficult tasks, difficult people, difficult times. Maybe we can learn to see these things as flowers instead of weeds and enjoy rather than dread them.

I've always enjoyed seeing a field covered with dandelions. I will try as well to enjoy the metaphorical weeds in my life. I may be surprised at the beauty and charm I find.

Courage and listening

> **"***Courage is what it takes to stand up and speak; courage is also what it takes to sit down and listen.***"**
>
> ➶ ANONYMOUS ➶

We stand behind our principles, and we're not afraid to tell people what we think. We've even gotten in trouble for that from time to time because people aren't always that interested in what we think.

What we may need to do a bit more of is to listen—really listen—to what others think and to give what they say serious consideration. Sometimes we're so busy planning the next thing that we want to say that we barely hear what anyone else has to offer.

I won't falter in my willingness to put myself on the line, but I realize that others may feel just as strongly about their positions. I will listen to and respect their thoughts—even if I still don't agree.

Taking responsibility

"God gives the nuts, but He does not crack them."
❧ GERMAN PROVERB ❧

If only the right opportunity were to come along, we think to ourselves, we could make a real success of things. We look with envy at others we see as being more successful. They must have gotten a big break somewhere along the way.

Chances are that we already have more opportunities than we realize. It's up to us to start recognizing these opportunities and taking advantage of them. This means actually working hard to turn opportunities into success.

Ultimately, the responsibility for my success is on me, no matter what circumstances I face or what difficulties I have to overcome.

Winning effort

> *"Winning is not everything, but the effort to win is."*
>
> ❧ ZIG ZIGLAR ☙

To run a marathon, we train for months. Although we may not expect to win, we hope at least to do well in our age group or to top a personal best. When the big day comes, we strive to meet whatever goal we've set for ourselves—to win, in other words, on our own terms. If we don't, are we losers? How could we be? We've worked hard, gotten into great shape, perhaps even made new friends. These things have more lasting importance than any transient rewards for crossing the finish line first.

It's great to set challenging goals for myself and then try to achieve them. Sometimes I will, but even when I don't, I'll have done some extraordinary work.

Ambition and happiness

" *When ambition ends, happiness begins.* **"**
HUNGARIAN PROVERB

A desire to get ahead seems natural. We want to be famous or rich or powerful or popular. We'd rather that others envy us than we envy others.

But ambition can cause us to focus so much on the goal ahead that we forget to enjoy what we've got right now. Maybe we're not the richest people we know, but we live pretty well. Maybe we're not the most popular person in the world, but we have friends who delight and support us.

I will do what I can to achieve my goals, but I won't let my ambition keep me from recognizing the good things I have in my life right now.

Giving

*"No person was ever honored for what he received.
Honor has been the reward for what he gave."*

CALVIN COOLIDGE

We're impressed by people who manage to give of themselves, even though they seem just as busy and overwhelmed as we are. Their willingness to help others, to exert themselves to make the world a better place, shows us what individuals can do, against considerable odds.

When I have opportunities to give, I'll take advantage of them. I will never regret having given of myself.

Expressing ourselves

"*Never express yourself more clearly than you are able to think.*"

❧ NIELS BOHR ❧

We've learned some good conversational skills over the years. We can even talk extensively on topics we know little about. Because we stand straight and speak without pausing, we convince everyone—maybe even ourselves—that we know what we're talking about.

Before we start giving off our "wisdom," we might want to take a few moments to consider whether we really know as much as we appear to. Maybe someone else, someone who's a little awkward in conversation, is the real expert on the topic being discussed.

My speaking skills may be polished, but that doesn't mean I have to use them all the time.

Hidden images

> "*A rock pile ceases to be a rock pile the moment a single man contemplates it, bearing within him the image of a cathedral.*"
>
> ❧ANTOINE DE SAINT-EXUPÉRY❧

The garden we think is a mess may be, to someone else, a rich example of natural plantings and nature's diversity. The man we find a crashing bore is, to the woman who loves him, a fountain of wise words and kindness.

Our perspective shapes everything—but we can open up the view if we want to. Once someone has pointed out the beauty of that messy garden, we may never see it the same way again. Once we look at the crashing bore through another lens, we, too, may see the wisdom and kindness.

My view of things is not the only way they can be seen. I will try to understand the perspectives of others and use them to widen my own.

Growth

"Happiness is neither virtue nor pleasure nor this thing nor that but simply growth. We are happy when we are growing."
❧ WILLIAM BUTLER YEATS ❧

Only humans "grow" in a way that means something more than adding to our dimensions. When we say we've grown, we mean we've had experiences, good and bad; we've learned lessons, painful and easy; we've opened ourselves to new things.

Growth isn't always easy—we have psychological growing pains at many times during our lives—but if we are not growing, we can't be truly happy.

I hope to grow in some way, every day of my life.

The right track

> "*Even if you are on the right track, you will get run over if you just sit there.*"
>
> ❧WILL ROGERS❧

We've got a plan, and it's a good one. Everything is ready. So . . . .

We sit and wait for life to start happening. Surely being poised and ready is enough. But, of course, it isn't. Just knowing where we want to go and preparing to go there isn't enough. At some point—sooner rather than later—we need to get moving. It's risky; things can go wrong. But there's really no alternative.

What steps can I take now to move towards my goals? I will do what it takes to act, to follow these steps, and to make things happen.

Work and play

> *"When you're following your energy and doing what you want all the time, the distinction between work and play dissolves."*
> SHAKTI GAWAIN

If we're lucky, we have work that is fulfilling and meaningful. We know people who tell us they can't wait to go to work each morning; the hours just fly by for them.

Not all of us have work that feels significant. But we can find ways to make our work more meaningful, no matter how humble or routine it is. What can we do that will benefit our coworkers? How can we do our job so that it challenges us in some way?

It's up to me to make my work satisfying. If I think that's impossible, what do I need to do to find work that will mean more to me?

Just one day

"*A single day is enough to make us a little larger or, another time, a little smaller.*"

PAUL KLEE

What can we do that matters in just one day? We can show kindness to someone, or we can make a stupid and mean remark that hurts someone. We can step forward when we see an injustice, big or small, or we can sit back quietly, afraid to get involved.

Every day we make decisions that determine what kind of people we are.

What can I do today to make a positive impact on someone or something?

Grabbing life

> *Life loves to be taken by the lapel and told:*
> *'I'm with you kid. Let's go.'*
>   **MAYA ANGELOU**

We often extol the virtues of planning, preparation, vision, cautiousness, and foresight. All of these things are important, but we're likely to miss out on opportunities if we don't, at least once in a while, just "go for it" and put caution aside.

I will embrace my life today, with everything I have.

Saying it hot

"Be still when you have nothing to say; when genuine passion moves you, say what you've got to say, and say it hot."

D.H. LAWRENCE

When people speak with true passion, we know it, we can feel it. We're drawn to them—a fact that good politicians understand. And when people sit quietly rather than making meaningless chitchat, their passion becomes even more apparent when they finally do express it.

When I have something to say, I will say it with strength and passion.

Truth and laughter

“*The absolute truth is the thing that makes
    people laugh.*”

❯ CARL REINER ❮

We all love a good joke of the "Knock, knock"
or "What do you get when you . . . ?" sort. But
what often makes us howl with laughter is hearing others tell a true story from their own life.

Telling funny stories about our mistakes and
embarrassing moments is a good way to put
them in perspective—and to keep our friends
amused.

I may or may not be good at telling jokes, but I
sure am good at making my life sound funny just
by telling the truth about the things I have done.

Preserving beauty

> **"***The real sin against life is to abuse and destroy beauty, even one's own—even more, one's own, for that has been put in our care and we are responsible for its well-being.***"**
> ❧KATHERINE ANNE PORTER☙

So many beautiful things have been given to us to protect, from the earth and all of its creatures, down to our own bodies.

We may not like how our toes look. Or how much we weigh. Or how our hair is thinning or going gray or, worse, both. But every movement of our bodies shows how beautifully designed they are. Every puff of wind and scent of flowers reminds us that we are fortunate to be on this planet, in this universe.

The earth is beautiful—and so am I. How can I make personal choices that protect the earth? How can I make choices that protect my own humanity?

Reflection

"*With an eye made quiet by the power of harmony, and the deep power of joy, we see into the life of things.*"

❧ WILLIAM WORDSWORTH ❧

We are constantly searching for knowledge, for answers to questions about the world we live in and the universe beyond. We wander through libraries, page through thick texts, spend hours at the computer, conduct painstaking research, and consult with experts.

Sometimes, in our search for knowledge, we also need to allow ourselves time for simple, quiet reflection. The answers that come to us in these moments may not be scientific, but they may help satisfy our deep longing to better understand the meaning of our lives.

I need to give myself time to reflect on my life. No directions, no "musts," no authorities—just quiet and thought.

Questions and answers

"You can tell whether a man is clever by his answers. You can tell whether a man is wise by his questions."

❧NAGUIB MAHFOUZ☙

We aren't crazy about know-it-alls. We may be impressed by the depth or breadth of their knowledge. We may have to concede that they are well educated. We may grudgingly acknowledge that they are clever.

But those who through their questions show that they are still searching for answers—that their minds are open to new ideas—often impress us more. They may hold strong opinions, but they listen to ours. They may talk about themselves, but they'd rather ask us to talk about ourselves.

I am smart enough to know that I don't know everything—and that asking good questions says a lot about what I do know.

Playing as a team

> "*The way a team plays as a whole determines its success. You may have the greatest bunch of individual stars in the world, but if they don't play together, the club won't be worth a dime.*"
> ❧BABE RUTH☙

We value individual skills, celebrating them with praise, awards, and money. But few achievements are entirely the work of a single individual. Most involve collaboration to some degree. Personal success depends not only on individual performance, but on the support of colleagues, friends, and family.

Learning how to use one's individual skills to work well in a group is a lifelong challenge. Luckily, it's also an enjoyable challenge. We can be proud when we have a personal success, but there's something especially wonderful about being part of a team that's successful.

I know how much I depend on the efforts and talents of those I work and play with.

Doing

"*I feel that the greatest reward for doing is the opportunity to do more.*"

❧JONAS SALK ❧

If we work faster and more efficiently than those around us, the odds are pretty good that we'll get more work to do. We may complain about this, but the truth is that we like to stay busy. The hours tick by at a painfully slow pace when we don't have enough to do, whether we're at work or at home.

Working, or doing, is one of the ways we define who we are. We need lots of work to feel purposeful and valued.

I'm grateful that I have things to do, even though I may complain that there's too much. Having too much to do is far better than having too little.

Autumn

*"Autumn is a second spring when every leaf
  is a flower."*

❧ALBERT CAMUS☙

The transitional seasons of spring and fall are
often times of transition in our personal lives as
well. We pack away clothes that are too heavy
or too light to wear—and pull out favorites from
the year before. We put up or take down screens
and storm windows; plant or harvest the garden;
move outdoor furniture in or out of the garage.

Fall is when school begins, always a good
time for fresh starts. Spring is when animals give
birth and people fall in love. (People fall in love
all year round, of course, but there's something
special about spring.)

I'll use this time before winter as if I were going
back to school. What do I want to accomplish this
year?

Compassion vs. indifference

" *The individual is capable of both great compassion and great indifference. He has it within his means to nourish the former and outgrow the latter.* "

❧NORMAN COUSINS❧

Compassion isn't something we're born with. Children generally are selfish beings. They learn compassion—if they do learn it—from others. "Why is that baby crying?" they wonder. Then they fall and bruise a knee, and they understand.

Learning compassion shouldn't stop in childhood. How often are we indifferent to the suffering of others, either blaming them for their own problems or ignoring them entirely? If we paid more attention, we could continue to learn compassion the way we did when we were very young.

However lucky I may be right now, I could be in need another time. I cannot be indifferent to others who are not as fortunate as me.

Being happy

"Now and then it's good to pause in our pursuit of happiness and just be happy."

GUILLAUME APOLLINAIRE

Happiness is more than just having good times. We spend a lot of money and effort looking for a good time—buying sports equipment, going out to eat, getting tickets to events. Activities like these can provide happiness, but they aren't the only things that will make us happy.

Rushing around to get to places and events can be stressful. And when we get the bills for these activities, our hearts can sink. We can be happy without spending money or rushing around—or even leaving the house—if we want to.

A happy day may mean staying home with people I love, enjoying simple pleasures that don't cost me anything.

A light from within

> *"People are like stained glass windows. They sparkle and shine when the sun is out, but when the darkness sets in, their true beauty is revealed only if there is a light from within."*
> ✒ELISABETH KÜBLER-ROSS✒

We know many people who are a delight to be around when things are going well. They're gracious and kind, funny and warm. We're happy to have them as friends.

We know fewer people who are equally delightful to be around when things aren't going so well. These special few manage to be gracious and kind, funny and warm, even when times are dark for them—and when we are suffering and needy and maybe not be such a delight ourselves.

I can be a good person in good times. I will strive to be a good person in difficult times as well.

Appreciation

> *"You have it easily in your power to increase the sum total of this world's happiness now. How? By giving a few words of sincere appreciation to someone who is lonely or discouraged. Perhaps you will forget tomorrow the kind words you say today, but the recipient may cherish them over a lifetime."*
>
> ❧ DALE CARNEGIE ❧

We've had our words come back to us, years later. We are embarrassed and rueful when we realize that something we said casually caused long-lasting hurt. And we're pleasantly surprised when we learn that a few positive words turned out to be exactly the solace someone needed. We didn't know that we could make so much difference in another person's life.

We need to be mindful of what we say—and what we fail to say.

I love it when someone says something positive to me. I will make sure I "pay that forward" and never hold back on offering encouraging and supportive words to others.

The right thing

"The truth of the matter is that you always know the right thing to do. The hard part is doing it."
❧ NORMAN SCHWARZKOPF ❧

Sometimes we waffle over what to do in a difficult situation simply because we're reluctant to do what we know we have to do. Maybe there's some sacrifice we don't really want to make. Maybe we're afraid we might alienate someone. Maybe we just don't want to put out the effort it's going to take.

So we procrastinate—asking for advice, weighing alternatives, hoping we'll find some way out of the situation. This is usually a futile exercise; we still have to do the right thing.

If I know what I have to do, I will do it rather than look for excuses not to. The satisfaction of knowing I've lived up to my own values will be worth any discomfort I might experience.

A work in progress

"We're all of us guinea pigs in the laboratory of God. Humanity is just a work in progress."
🖎 TENNESSEE WILLIAMS 🖎

If there's a plan to things, why do we seem to be in such a mess? Wars, disease, famine, environmental damage, poverty—the list goes on and one. Surely we can do better.

If we think of ourselves, and all of humanity, as a work in progress, we might be more forgiving of others—and more hopeful of what will come in the future.

The idea that human beings can improve, individually and globally, cheers me.

Living in the moment

> *"The secret of health for both mind and body is not to mourn for the past, not to worry about the future, or not to anticipate troubles, but to live in the present moment wisely and earnestly."*
>
> **✎ BUDDHA ✎**

From moment to moment, our thoughts want to drift away from the present, backwards to the past or forwards to the future. The allure may be the rosy glow of a nostalgic past or the bright promise of a better future. Or, in darker moods, we may punish ourselves with memories of past mistakes or fears of unrealized troubles.

What we lose when we focus on the past or the future is the reality of now, this moment— the only time we truly have. And we are very lucky to have it.

I will enjoy this moment, just as it is. I will live in this moment, just as it is.

Voices within

"The more faithfully you listen to the voices within you, the better you will hear what is sounding outside."

❧ DAG HAMMARSKJOLD ☙

Listening to the radio or watching television, we constantly encounter opinions from people who seem pretty sure of themselves. Newspapers and magazines are full of columns from experts on every topic imaginable.

And then there are our friends, family members, and coworkers, all eager to dispense advice. Our head is filled with the noise of all these opinions, noise that sometimes only confuses us. Our opinions can be informed by these other voices, but the one voice we always need to hear is our own.

I value the opinions of others, both experts and people I know and respect. But I am a reasonable person with gut feelings that also need to be heeded.

A right to be wrong

> *"A child becomes an adult when he realizes that he has a right not only to be right but also to be wrong."*
>
> ❧THOMAS SZASZ❧

We get to be wrong sometimes. Sure, there may well be consequences to being wrong. We may look stupid or incompetent. We may need to atone for something we've said or done. But being wrong is an inescapable aspect of being human.

I don't want to be wrong, but I understand that it's okay if I am sometimes. Nothing requires that I be right all the time. If I were, I would be one very extraordinary person—or a very deluded one.

Learning

"*Learning is a treasure that will follow its owner everywhere.*"

❧ CHINESE PROVERB ❧

Some of us have spent years in school. Some of us have shelves full of books. Some of us seek the advice and counsel of experts. Some of us try to find answers to questions on our own.

We stop learning when we stop asking questions and looking for the answers. We never need to stop learning.

I don't think of learning as a formal education but as something I do every day.

Our senses

“*Nothing we use or hear or touch can be expressed in words that equal what we are given by the senses.*”

⤮ HANNAH ARENDT ⤯

Words are the way we connect with others; they are very powerful things. But they can't fully communicate what we experience every day just by being in the world. The sound of the birds outside our window. The warmth of the sun coming through a window and resting on the back of our neck. The complex, somewhat bitter taste of a cup of coffee. The smell of bread baking in the oven.

We can describe these things to others, but they will only know them through their own sensory experiences. Our senses bring us the world in intensely personal ways.

My senses are powerful. I will take time today to see, hear, touch, taste, and smell my world.

Wilderness of intuition

"You have to leave the city of your comfort and go into the wilderness of your intuition. What you'll discover will be wonderful. What you'll discover is yourself."

ALAN ALDA

We gravitate towards comfort. We might have some complaints about our lives—things aren't perfect—but we know who we are and where we're going (more or less), and we feel okay about it.

What happens when we step out of our comfort zone? Spending a year in another country can cause us to see ourselves and the world much differently. A great loss—or any major change—can push us into a place we never imagined.

I need to step out of my comfort zone and see what happens. Rather than fight change, I'll embrace it.

Human imagination

"Nature uses human imagination to lift her work of creation to even higher levels."

LUIGI PIRANDELLO

We live in a marvelous world, made all the more marvelous by the creations of human imagination. A beautiful landscape is enhanced and preserved in a painting. Even when we are far from it, the beauty of that landscape—and the particular moment in time that it was captured by the artist—can be recalled simply by looking at the painting.

I enjoy both the natural world and the creations of human imagination that reflect it.

Studying the stars

"I try to forget what happiness was, and when that don't work, I study the stars."

◆ DEREK WALCOTT ◆

When our lives are troubled and the future looks bleak, we can always step out into the night and look up into the sky. The stars never fail to humble us—we are so tiny, so insignificant in the great scheme of things—and to remind us how much beauty and wonder there is in the universe.

I look at the stars and feel I am a part of something magnificent. I don't understand it, but I am in awe.

Willing change

"*It is not by spectacular achievements that man can be transformed, but by will.*"

HENRIK IBSEN

How do we change ourselves? How do we change the world? We hope for saviors, for magic, for something wonderful that will bring peace and understanding, that will end hunger, that will give children everywhere the chance to grow up safe.

While we hope for saviors and magic, we also must set our will and do what we can on our own to make a difference.

I'm not sure what I can do to change the world and help make it better, but I'll find something. If each of us does one small thing, the world will change.

Attitude and success

    "*It is our attitude at the beginning of a difficult task which, more than anything else, will affect its successful outcome.*"

        ❧ WILLIAM JAMES ❧

We've all made the excuses: We can't do it. It's too hard. It's boring. It takes too much time. It's not worth the trouble.

    When we begin difficult tasks with attitudes like these, we are destined to fail. Even if we can't change a particular task, we can change the way we look at it. Yes, it's hard, but we can do it. We just need to make the commitment.

I want to succeed whenever possible. I will make sure my attitude doesn't undermine my chances.

Believing

> "*More persons, on the whole, are humbugged by believing in nothing than by believing in too much.*"
>
> P. T. BARNUM

Which is better: to believe in something or someone and to suffer disappointment once in a while, or to doubt everything and everyone and never be disappointed?

Cynics and pessimists aren't usually happy people. Perhaps their expectations are self-fulfilling; the people, causes, and institutions they expect to disappoint them generally do. When we take the risk of believing—and it is a risk—we also take a chance on finding happiness.

I am a risk-taker. I will let myself believe.

Exploration

> "*If a man will begin with certainties, he shall end in doubts, but if he will be content to begin with doubts, he shall end in certainties.*"
>
> ❧ SIR FRANCIS BACON ❧

We know what the right thing to do is. Don't bother arguing with us about it; we're certain. So we begin with this certainty and—suddenly, there's a fork in the road that's not on the map. What do we do now? We choose a path, and it's the wrong one. Now we're lost, and we're not sure how to get back to where we need to be.

If we had been less sure of ourselves, we might have done a better job of preparing for the unexpected, or asked people we met along the way for advice. Then, when we reached the fork in the road, we might have known which way to turn.

Even when I'm sure—especially when I'm sure—I know exactly what I'm doing, I will be open to advice and information from others.

Wanting things

"I do not read advertisements. I would spend all of my time wanting things."

⟨ FRANZ KAFKA ⟩

We live surrounded by things: electronic devices, appliances, clothing, books, music, pictures, furniture, utensils, tools, and knickknacks of all sorts. Yet most of us crave more. And when we get more, we want even more.

We're bombarded with messages telling us that we're not complete until we have this thing or that thing or more of these things or newer versions of those things. It takes a strong will to resist the pressure to consume.

I don't need more things to make myself happy. Can I spend a week without buying any new thing? A month? Longer?

Activity

“*The really idle man gets nowhere. The perpetually busy man does not get much further.*”

❬❬ SIR HENEAGE OGILIVIE ❬❬

We sometimes feel overwhelmed by the demands on our time. Our calendar is stuffed with meetings, lunches, parties, and other activities and obligations. Just looking at our schedule can make us feel anxious and exhausted.

We tend to spend too much time on things that neither make us happy nor advance us towards our goals—and too little time in activities that enhance our lives and bring us closer to what we want.

I can simplify my calendar, canceling some of those events that aren't as essential as I thought when I penciled them in. What can I do this week that really delights me? This is what should be in my calendar.

Pardons

"We are all full of weakness and errors;
let us mutually pardon each other our follies;
it is the first law of nature."

❧ VOLTAIRE ☙

If we accepted that other people are flawed—
and that their flaws can even make them more
interesting—and if they accepted us with all of
our flaws, our days would be so much easier.

We curse the driver who swerves in front of
us. We are annoyed by the clerk who doesn't
wait on us quickly enough. Our friends and
family members are always falling short of
our expectations. We spend a lot of time with
clenched jaws thinking about others' shortcomings. How much more productive might
we be if we focused on more positive things?

I'm going to spend a day thinking only good things
about the people around me and see how that
feels.

Opportunities to learn

"It is always in season for old men to learn."
AESCHYLUS

Every day is an opportunity to learn something new. Reading a newspaper. Listening to the radio. Talking with friends. Taking a class. Or just watching what's going on around us.

We regularly encounter things that we can learn from—if we would just open our eyes to them. What if we were to really pay attention to the world around us? What if we were to ask more questions? What if we were to seek out answers to these questions? Even if the answers only confirmed what we already knew, the search would help keep us sharper and more engaged.

I want to be a permanent student because it keeps me engaged with life—and makes me a more interesting person.

Life and onions

> "*Life is like an onion; you peel it off one layer at a time and sometimes you weep.*"
> ❧ CARL SANDBURG ☙

We can't know everything about life, no matter how much we study and reflect. There will always be mystery.

What we can do is enjoy each stage as we go through life, knowing that another, perhaps very different stage, will follow. We may have difficult times, but they are likely to be followed by happy and productive times.

I enjoy the different periods of my life, even the bad ones, because I know that they shape the person that I am and the story that I tell.

Pluses and minuses

"I'm treating you as a friend, asking you to share my present minuses in the hope that I can ask you to share my future pluses."
KATHERINE MANSFIELD

Asking someone for help and support—or even accepting help and support that we didn't ask for—honors the other person. We are all vulnerable in one way or another, and we rely on our friends not to exploit our vulnerabilities. We trust them to accept both our pluses and minuses.

Offering trust means offering friendship as well.

I am lucky to have friends who let me cry on their shoulders without becoming impatient—and who laugh with me when I'm joyful.

Inaction

> *"Throughout history, it has been the inaction of those who could have acted, the indifference of those who should have known better, the silence of the voice of justice when it matter most, that has made it possible for evil to triumph."*
>
> ❧HAILE SELASSIE☙

A very few people can do very great harm if the rest of us just sit back and let them. When we're not the ones being directly harmed, it's especially easy to rationalize inaction. Okay, we don't like what's happening, but what can we do? It doesn't affect us, anyway, right?

Just as it only takes a small number doing harm to bring evil into the world, it only takes a small number actively resisting to stop them.

It's not enough for me to be good to others. I need to stand up to those who harm others.

Looking back

"What is now proved was only once imagined."
William Blake

A man on the moon? That was the stuff of fiction—until it happened. Instant communication with people around the world? We don't think twice about what a miracle that is, because we're so used to it.

There are things that seem absurd or impossible today that we—or our children and grandchildren—will find perfectly ordinary in the future.

I take so many aspects of daily life for granted. For just a moment, I'll stop to think about how amazing the modern world is—and how much I depend on its technology.

Running

"All men should strive to learn before they die,
what they are running from, and to, and why."
JAMES THURBER

We think of ourselves as running towards things—love, prosperity, happiness. What makes us run towards these things? Or is it really that we are running away from our past? Does it matter?

It's good to understand why we want the things we want, to make sure our reasons are sound—and that what we're trying to accomplish is right for us.

I have goals that I work towards. I won't take my goals for granted. Every so often, I need to look hard at why I want what I want—and to make changes if necessary.

Miracles

"We shall find peace.
We shall hear angels.
We shall see the sky sparkling with diamonds."
❧ANTON CHEKOV☙

Whatever our faith, a belief in miracles helps us enjoy everyday life. Miracles can be as ordinary—and wonderful—as a drop of rain, the birth of a child, or a moment of quiet.

I live amid miracles.

Friendship

"A true friend is the greatest of all blessings, and that which we take the least care to acquire."
🙰FRANÇOIS DE LA ROCHEFOUCAULD🙰

We don't typically set out to make a friend the same way we set out to get a job or win the attention of someone we're attracted to. Friends just seem to happen. We work or play together, discover that we share some things in common, and gradually a friendship grows. Or we face some hardship or misfortune together, and a friendship arises through mutual support.

We make friends casually, but once they're part of our lives, we should be careful not to take them for granted. Our friends make us better, stronger, and happier—and we should do the same for them.

I remember every day how lucky I am in my friendships. Today I'm going to tell my friends how much I appreciate them.

Confidence

"I figured that if I said it enough, I would convince the world that I really was the greatest."
≈MUHAMMAD ALI≈

We walk into the room, head held high, a confident smile on our face. Everything about us tells people that we're someone they would want to know. When we start with a confident attitude, we are almost irresistible.

There's an expression, "Fake it till you make it," which means to act the part until we become it. If we don't feel confident, we can still fake it until we make it. And we will make it.

If I act like the confident person I want to be, not only will others perceive me as confident, I will become more confident.

Reality

> **"**We must have strong minds, ready to accept facts as they are.**"**
>
> **◆ HARRY S. TRUMAN ◆**

Reality is rough. The world isn't as we would like it to be. Times are hard. And we'd really rather not have to think about things, thank you very much.

To avoid facing reality, we sugarcoat the facts for ourselves and others. But reality has a way of catching up to us. Ultimately, reality is a lot easier to face when we recognize it and deal with it right away.

I can deal with reality even when I don't like it.

Listening

"Listening, not imitation, may be the sincerest form of flattery."

☙DR. JOYCE BROTHERS☙

We are drawn to people who understand us. And how do we know we're understood? Because people who understand us ask us questions, listen to the answers, encourage us to elaborate, and respond directly to what we say.

Real attention is one of the nicest and most meaningful things we can give anyone. We don't do it often enough.

I want to make sure that I listen to others carefully and sincerely. It will make them feel good—and I can learn a lot, too.

Active voice

"*We have not passed that subtle line between childhood and adulthood until we move from the passive voice to the active voice—that is, until we have stopped saying, 'It got lost,' and say, 'I lost it.'*"

❧ SYDNEY J. HARRIS ❧

Accepting responsibility for one's missteps and wrong decisions is a basic principle for leading an ethical life. But just a few minutes of watching the news reveals how seldom people take responsibility for their actions. Too many people of authority and power speak as if they have neither, as if things just happen to them.

We understand why this is. Who wants to admit they've done something wrong in front of others? Yet we know that it's the right thing to do.

I will take responsibility for what I do. When I make a mistake, I'll admit it.

Thinking

> *"A great many people think they are thinking when they are merely rearranging their prejudices."*
> **EDWARD R. MURROW**

Isn't it funny how we can come up with new reasons to support the same argument we've been making for years? We all operate a little bit like lawyers, knowing what we want others to believe (our client is not guilty) and continually figuring out different ways to argue for this (he wasn't there; if he was there, he didn't do it; if he did it, it was an accident).

If we were to seriously consider new ideas rather than simply rearrange old ideas, we might discover new ways to think.

I'm open to new ideas, even when they challenge my strongest beliefs.

Doing more

"Do a little more each day than you think you possibly can."

⮡LOWELL THOMAS⮠

Even during our busiest days, there's usually a little more we can do. We can get up a bit earlier or stay up a little later. We can pay less attention to distractions and more attention to things that really matter. We can, in short, be more careful about how we spend our time.

It feels good to get to the end of the day and realize that we've accomplished more than we set out to do. We go to bed satisfied and wake up ready to do even more the next day.

I know I can do more today—and everyday. I will push myself a little—and I'll be glad I did.

Reading

"Of all the diversions of life, there is none so proper to fill up its empty spaces as the reading of useful and entertaining authors."
≈ JOSEPH ADDISON ≈

When we want to visit faraway places but lack the money to travel, we can read. When we want to forget that the weather is wet and cold and we're bored, we can read. When we want to learn something new or develop a skill, we can read.

In an age of television, the Internet, video games, and more, we sometimes forget that for little or no money, and with just a little imagination, we can explore other worlds and learn from history's greatest minds without ever leaving our house.

I will try more often to reach for a book instead of the television remote control.

Our mission

"*Here is a test to find out whether your mission on earth is finished: If you are alive, it isn't.*"

RICHARD BACH

When do we no longer have to be concerned about improving ourselves and the world we live in? When can we just sit back and do—well, nothing? The answer—as long as we're alive—is never. We might as well ask when we no longer need to breathe or think or feel. We need to remain engaged with the world for as long as we are able to do so.

I hope I never lose the drive to attain understanding, wisdom, and happiness.

Our weaknesses

> *"Once we know our own weaknesses they cease to do us any harm."*
> ❧ GEORG CHRISTOPH LICHTENBERG ❧

We get in trouble more often because of what we don't know about ourselves than what we do know. Oblivious to our limits, we attempt things we can't really handle. Unaware that we have an annoying habit of taking over conversations, we drive away potential friendships. Blind to the assumptions we make about people who are different from us, we miss opportunities to learn and expand our horizons.

It's not easy to face our weaknesses, but when we do face them, we have a chance to correct or work around them.

Am I aware of all my weaknesses? Maybe some of my closest friends will—gently—help me identify them so I can change, if I want to.

Survival of the species

"It is not the strongest of the species that survive, nor the most intelligent, but the one most responsive to change."

— CHARLES DARWIN —

Research has shown that those who are happiest in old age are the ones who have dealt most successfully with the changes in their lives. Learning to accept and adapt to change is the skill of a lifetime.

Because there is never a shortage of changes for us to face, we should have plenty of opportunities to practice our adaptive skills—and to get very good at them.

I've already faced many changes in my life. Which changes have I handled well? And what can I learn from these experiences to help me deal with change in the future?

Humility

"Humility is the only true wisdom by which we prepare our minds for all the possible changes of life."

❧ GEORGE ARLISS ❧

Being humble is not the same as lacking confidence. Humility means acknowledging that we have limits, that we need support and guidance from others, that we cannot go it completely alone. We can have great confidence in ourselves while still understanding that it is impossible to be totally self-reliant in this complex, challenging, and rapidly changing world.

If we acknowledge that we can't manage everything by ourselves, we are more likely to ask for help from others—and achieve success.

I'm a competent person, but I know I can't do everything myself. I will not be shy about asking for help when I need it.

The value of work

"No labor, however humble, is dishonoring."
❧ THE TALMUD ❧

We should never be embarrassed about our work or look down our noses at the work of others. If anything is embarrassing, it is to do a job poorly that we are perfectly capable of doing well.

Not all work is compensated with money or occurs in a traditional workplace. Whether we are mining for coal, performing surgery, taking care of children, or cooking dinner for those we love, our work brings us its own rewards, beyond the immediate needs it fulfills.

I value my work and respect the work of others.

Time for home

> "Winter is the time for comfort, for good food and
> warmth, for the touch of a friendly hand and for
> a talk beside the fire: It is the time for home."
>   **DAME EDITH SITWELL**

We may think of winter as a time of coldness,
grayness, and darkness, even if we live in a
temperate climate. However, there's another
way to look at this often maligned season. It's
a time when we gather together to create our
own light and warmth—a time of holidays and
special occasions. Many of our best memories
are of cozy winter evenings spent with family
and friends.

I will enjoy winter, getting together with those I
love and smiling at their bright faces.

Real beauty

66*You can only perceive real beauty in a person as they get older.*99

≈ ANOUK AIMÉE ≈

Youth has its own special appeal. Young eyes are bright, young skin is taut and dewy, young bodies are limber and quick.

But beauty—real beauty—requires something youth does not have. Beauty is not simply a youthful glow or collection of attractive features. It may, in fact, be just the opposite. Real beauty blooms from the soil of experience, knowledge, and wisdom. It is more a reflection of inner attitudes than a physical image in a mirror.

What will I look like as I get older? What does my face show now? Will I perceive the real beauty in myself and others?

Studying history

"*We can chart our future clearly and wisely only when we know the path which has led to the present.*"

ADLAI E. STEVENSON

We didn't just arrive at this point in our lives; we have a history. What brought us to this place? What things did we do along the way that turned out to be mistakes, and what things turned out to be wise?

Before we make plans for where we want to go next, it's good to look back at the journey we've already taken. We don't have to repeat the same mistakes. Instead, we can use the best ideas we've had in the past to map our way into the future.

I'll use my past as a guide to what I will do next.

Facts and opinions

> **❝***It is not the facts which guide the conduct of men, but their opinions about facts, which may be entirely wrong. We can only make them right by discussion.***❞**
>
> ❧ NORMAN ANGELL ❧

If facts were all it took to get people to agree, newspaper editorial pages would disappear. One person argues a position eloquently, based on a set of facts. The next day, someone else argues a different position, equally eloquently, based on the same set of facts.

We look at facts from our own perspective, using them to bolster what we already believe. If we talk with those who disagree, often what we explore is not facts but perspectives. This can be a good thing, because we can't change facts, but we can change our perspectives.

I have to remember that as strongly as I believe something, and as much as I think that anyone seeing the same facts would believe the same thing, there are other perspectives.

Wit

"Wit is the only wall between us and the dark."
☙ MARK VAN DOREN ☙

Without humor—without the ability to make fun of ourselves and the situations we find ourselves in—the world would be a very bleak place. With a twist of irony we can turn the bad things that happen to us into amusing stories. And as we tell and retell these stories, we remind ourselves that we can bear almost anything that life can throw at us.

I will use my humor to get me through difficult times.

First attempts

*" It doesn't matter how many say it cannot be done
or how many people have tried it before;
it's important to realize that whatever you're
doing, it's your first attempt at it. "*

❧ WALLY AMOS ❧

People offer to share their experiences with us,
and this can be helpful. But sometimes other
people's experiences can hold us back from
trying things that we might otherwise succeed
at. No, people tell us, don't even try. This thing
can't be done. These people know; they've tried
themselves. Or they *think* they know, even when
they haven't tried themselves.

But maybe we will do this thing differently—
just differently enough to succeed. Or maybe
we'll make mistakes that no one else has ever
made before, and these mistakes will show us
(or others) how to succeed. In any case we'll
give ourselves credit for trying.

I get to try things on my own, even if others have
failed or tried to discourage me.

Problem-solving

"The 'how' thinker gets problems solved effectively because he wastes no time with futile 'ifs.'"
NORMAN VINCENT PEALE

We can usually come up with a lot of reasons for not attempting to solve a particular problem. The solution will cost too much, not everyone is on board with it, it's just a temporary fix. There are so many "ifs," we fret and stew and do nothing.

In the meantime, someone else is taking action. Maybe this action will solve the problem, maybe not. But we can never solve any problem unless we try.

While it's important to consider the potential consequences of any action, I can't let the "ifs" paralyze me into inaction.

A lifetime

> *"How far you go in life depends on your being tender with the young, compassionate with the aged, sympathetic with the striving, and tolerant of the weak and strong. Because someday in your life you will have been all of these."*
>
> ~ GEORGE WASHINGTON CARVER ~

We often think, as we get older, that if we'd known what we know now, we would have treated our elders differently when we were younger. Conversely, as we age, we can forget what it is like to think, feel, and act like a child. When we're successful, we can become blind to how hard life can be for those who are still struggling. And when we master a skill, we may have little tolerance for those who aren't equally adept.

Wherever I am in my life's journey, I can be tender, compassionate, sympathetic, and tolerant towards those who are at a different place in their journey.

Intention

*"Others have seen what is and asked why.
I have seen what could be and asked why not."*
ROBERT F. KENNEDY

The first step to accomplishing any task is
believing that we can. We begin with this belief
and then figure out what we need to do to
complete the task.

But believing in our ability to accomplish
something sometimes requires considerable will.
For one reason or another, there may be many
voices telling us we can't or shouldn't attempt a
particular task. If we listen to these voices, we
have failed before we even try.

I will believe in my ability to do what needs to be
done, and I will figure out a way to do it.

Changing

"*The main dangers in this life are the people who want to change everything or nothing.*"
❧LADY NANCY ASTOR☙

Extreme revolutionaries want to change everything. They see nothing of value worth preserving. Extreme conservatives resist change of any kind. They believe that things are just the way they should be.

Neither extreme is realistic or productive. It's impossible to freeze the world exactly as it is for any length of time. And even if we could prevent change, the result would be stifling. On the other hand, as much as we might want to change everything about our lives and start fresh, we would still be who we are—flaws and all. Better to look for those things in our life that are worth preserving and to build on them.

Change is always happening, and I can embrace it rather than resist or ignore it.

Celebration

"I celebrate myself, and sing myself."
❧ WALT WHITMAN ☙

Let's try saying something as simple and powerful as "I celebrate myself." It's a bit unusual, perhaps even embarrassing, isn't it? Sounds kind of egotistical. When others celebrate us, it feels pretty good, but to celebrate ourselves . . . ?

Children enjoy celebrating themselves. When a baby first finds her own toes, she is completely delighted. When a toddler realizes that he can make sounds that bring him rewards, he beams proudly. Why can't we take a similar delight in the simple wonder of being alive? Our life is a great gift worth celebrating.

At least once each day, I will offer a quiet celebration of the miracle that is me.

Sharing joy

"The sharing of joy, whether physical, emotional, psychic, or intellectual, forms a bridge between the sharers which can be the basis for understanding much of what is not shared between them, and lessens the threat of their difference."

❧ AUDRE LORD ❧

We feel good about the people with whom we share good times—a joke, a great movie, an enjoyable trip. Sharing good times gives us reasons to want to know others better, even if we have a lot of differences. Maybe we vote for different candidates, live in different places, care about different things. Still, because we have done something joyful together, we are more willing to accept and respect our differences, rather than simply dismiss each other because we don't have much in common.

The more opportunities I have to do enjoyable things with others, especially people I may not know well, the better I can understand those who are different from me.

Kindness at home

"If you have only one smile in you, give it to the
people you love. Don't be surly at home, then
go out in the street and start grinning 'Good
morning' at total strangers."

MAYA ANGELOU

We put on our "outside faces" when we meet
people outside our home. We exchange small
talk with the clerk at the store, nod and smile at
everyone we pass on the street, say "Don't worry
about it" to someone who's just bumped into us.
We're just being polite, we think.

At home we drop the polite face because
home is where we can be ourselves, right? We
grumble and maybe even snap. We don't bother
to smile because these people love us anyway.
Why can't we treat friends and family as well as
people we don't even know?

I will treat those closest to me with the same
courtesy I treat strangers. My loved ones and I
will be much happier.

Building character

"Character builds slowly, but it can be torn down with incredible swiftness."

⮌ FAITH BALDWIN ⮍

We can be both strong and fragile at the same time. This is one of the paradoxes of human existence. Sometimes, we seem capable of bearing almost anything. Other times, a few harsh words can tear us apart. Maybe this is why we often wonder if we're really as good or as strong as we think we are.

A basic kindness we can do for others is to help them protect their own sense of strength and value.

I will always try to help build, not destroy, self-esteem in others—and in myself.

Sweet, simple things

"*I am beginning to learn that it is the sweet, simple things of life which are the real ones after all.***"**
LAURA INGALLS WILDER

A baby's giggle, the warmth of flannel sheets, a favorite meal—the simple things can bring us much happiness.

We enjoy these simple things for what they are, but also for what they evoke: people we have loved, times of peace and contentment, the promise the future holds.

If I make a list of things that make me happy, few of the items will be extravagant.

Looking like a winner

❝*Regardless of how you feel inside, always try
to look like a winner. Even if you are behind, a
sustained look of control and confidence can give
you a mental edge that results in victory.*❞
ARTHUR ASHE

Dress the part, act the part—and you might just
get the part. Looking and acting confident helps
convince others that we are capable of doing
what we say we can do.

Sometimes, though, we first have to convince
ourselves of our competence. Fortunately, the
same principle applies. If we can put on the
right clothes *and* the right attitude, we can be as
confident as we look.

If I don't feel confident, I will make a special effort
to create the appearance of confidence. That may
mean putting on a particular outfit, one in which I
feel I'm at my best. It definitely means putting on
a confident attitude.

Dealing with fortune

"Has fortune dealt you some bad cards?
Then let wisdom make you a good gamester."
☙ FRANCIS QUARLES ☙

One person with a history of bad luck still finds ways to succeed, while another in a similar situation manages only a long, sad story about why success is impossible. The difference between the two is what they make of what they have.

Some of us may have to work twice as hard as others to accomplish the same things. Is this fair? No. But rather than wasting our energy by complaining, why not try to figure out how to get what we want in spite of the lack of fairness?

When the odds are stacked against me, even though I've done nothing to deserve my bad luck, I won't let myself feel frustrated. Instead, I'll figure out what I need to do to beat the odds.

Something to help

"Everybody wants to do something to help, but nobody wants to be the first."

PEARL BAILEY

We're so afraid of doing the wrong thing, of embarrassing ourselves or the person we want to help, that we stand back until others have stepped forward. Now it's safe for us to do something. We can see what others are doing and follow in their steps.

If everyone were to act this way, no one would ever get the help they need. We admire those people who pick up a shovel or bake a casserole or write a check and just do something when they see someone else in need.

If someone I know needs help, I'm not going to wait to provide it. I may be wrong about what kind of help is needed sometimes, but that's not as bad as doing nothing when help is needed.

Sympathy

" There is nothing sweeter than to be
sympathized with. "
❧ GEORGE SANTAYANA ❧

"I'm so sorry. If there's anything I can do, please tell me." We love the person who says this to us. No long recitations of that person's own problems, no unasked for advice, just an affirmation that someone else understands who we are and why we feel the way we do.

We don't want pity; we want sympathy. We want to be recognized. And we want our circumstances to be recognized. That's all—but it's everything.

If someone I know is in trouble, I'll listen—really listen. I want to hear what the person says so I can understand what is going on and be honestly sympathetic.

Facing problems

> ❝*Not everything that is faced can be changed,*
> *but nothing can be changed until it is faced.*❞
> ❧JAMES BALDWIN❧

"Admitting the problem is the first step towards change" may sound corny, but it is often true. We can't do better until we admit that we're not doing well.

We're all pretty good at trying to hide or ignore a problem for as long as possible. Maybe it's just a temporary thing, we think. Maybe it's not that bad, and no one else has noticed. Maybe it's not a problem at all; everyone else does it, too. When we argue with ourselves or others that a problem isn't really a problem, the chances are, it really is a problem.

I'll try to be honest with myself about my own problems and shortcomings. I may not be able to change all of them, but I can't change any of them until I admit they exist.

Freedom and control

"*To enjoy freedom we have to control ourselves.*"
VIRGINIA WOOLF

Freedom is easily lost. We want to be free, but we also want to be safe, and sometimes the two don't seem compatible. The wilder we are in our freedom, the less safe others may feel—which can lead to restrictions that leave us less free.

We live this odd irony: To be free, we have to be careful not to be *too* free.

I enjoy great freedom in my daily life, which I protect by using wisely.

Doing all the talking

"*Never fail to know that if you are doing all the talking, you are boring somebody.*"
—HELEN GURLEY BROWN

When we're out with others, engaged in conversation, we are involved in a kind of theater. First we say something, then they say something. We watch their reaction to us and adjust our performance accordingly. Are they laughing when we say something amusing, or are they distracted by something in another part of the room? Are they making eye contact with us, or are they looking down at the floor as we speak?

If, on occasion, we forget that this is an interactive drama, not a monologue, we may find ourselves looking into the glazed eyes and yawning mouth of a person trying to get away from us without seeming rude.

I have some great stories to tell—and so do the people I want to tell them to. I need to make room for them on the "stage" of our conversation.

Together

> 66 *These are the same stars, and that is the same moon, that look down upon your brothers and sisters, and which they see as they look up to them, though they are ever so far away from us, and each other.* 99
>
> 🖎 SOJOURNER TRUTH 🖎

The universe is too big for us to imagine—and expanding more all the time. We look at blinking stars and know that what we see took place thousands of years in the past.

The night sky, wherever we are, unites us with the rest of the world—and the rest of human history. The sky changes constantly, and yet seems unchanged. It is, in many ways, the same sky depicted in early drawings and on the maps of men setting out on the waters of a world they thought was flat.

Looking at the stars is a powerful reminder of how beautiful and mysterious our universe is and how connected we all are.

Good deeds

"*Keep doing good deeds long enough and you'll probably turn out a good man in spite of yourself.*"

❧LOUIS AUCHINCLOSS☙

We sometimes doubt our own goodness because we have mean thoughts or fail to seize opportunities to be kind to others. We worry that if others really knew who we are deep inside, perhaps they wouldn't think we were very good at all, so we may do good deeds partly in order to appear good to others.

But if no one else can see deep inside us— if others see only our good deeds—what does "deep inside" mean? Does it matter?

If I do good things for people—even if I do them because I think I ought to and not because my heart leaps to do them—I am still a good person.

Mercy and justice

66*Among the attributes of God, although they are
equal, mercy shines with even more brilliance
than justice.*99

❧ MIGUEL DE CERVANTES SAAVEDRA ❧

All faith traditions incorporate ideals of justice
and mercy. We, as representatives of our faith,
are drawn to both ideals. We crave the order and
sanity that the ideal of justice brings: Those who
harm others should be punished; those who
have been harmed should receive reparation.

Even more, we crave the redemption that the
ideal of mercy brings: We may not be perfect,
we may make mistakes, but we should be given
the opportunity to do better.

When I am wronged, my first instinct is to want
some kind of justice. I will be a better person
if I can show mercy towards the person who
wronged me.

Making mistakes

> *"If I had my life to live again, I'd make the same mistakes, only sooner."*
> ❧TALLULAH BANKHEAD☙

Mistakes can make us more interesting than the things we do right. We may cause pain to ourselves or others, hamper our professional progress, or just plain embarrass ourselves. But, oh, what we learn from our mistakes!

I don't set out to make mistakes, but I make them anyway. But I have to admit, now that some time has gone by, some of my mistakes have been a lot of fun.

Moral power

> "*Moral power is probably best when it is not used. The less you use it, the more you have.*"
> ◆ANDREW YOUNG◆

When we think we're right, we think we're right. We're convinced that what we believe, and what we want done, is supported by moral authority. And we want to use this moral authority to force others to believe as we believe. But even though others may sometimes do what we want, they don't always seem very happy about it.

Any power, even moral power—perhaps especially moral power—can create resentment. None of us want to be ordered or coerced. We want to feel that we've looked at a situation and made our own choices.

Even when I'm right, and there's no question about it, I'll do better if I try to win others over to my position, rather than forcing them to do what I want.

Intimacy

" The easiest kind of relationship is with ten thousand people, the hardest is with one. "

◈ JOAN BAEZ ◈

Everyone at the office loves us. They think we're funny and warm and always so supportive. So why are we having trouble getting along with the person closest to us?

We show our most vulnerable self to the person we care most about. That can make us prickly and nervous. What if we're rejected? What if we lose the person we care about? Or the opposite: We try hard to win the attention and admiration of those at the office, while we take our loved one for granted because we know we already have his or her attention, admiration, and love.

I recognize that my closest relationships take the most care. A close relationship can be one of my most rewarding experiences, and one of my most difficult.

Keeping on

"The race is not always to the swift, but to those who keep on running."

ANONYMOUS

In life, even more than in fables, what counts is that we keep going, despite the obstacles in front of us. There are plenty of examples of what happens to those who win fame, fortune, or power too quickly. All we have to do is browse the magazines at the supermarket to see them.

Most of us won't have our lives chronicled in print, but we will have lives of value. We'll love others, do the best we can, and just keep getting out of bed every morning and going about our daily business.

There are many things I'd like to accomplish—or wish I had accomplished already. I won't be frustrated by not having done everything I aspire to. I'll just keep working at it.

Consequences of anger

> *"How much more grievous are the consequences of anger than the causes of it."*
> ❧ MARCUS AURELIUS ☙

*I*t's possible to have an ongoing feud with some-one and then realize, after days or months or even years, that we don't remember what we were feuding over in the first place. In the meantime, we've said terrible things to each other, maybe even had a few fights.

People sometimes hurt us, deliberately or not, in ways we feel justify our anger. But justified anger can be as harmful as unjustified anger. We can't do anything about other people and what they do; we can only change what we do. We can learn to release our anger.

I may not be able to avoid getting angry at times, but I can get past it and move on. When I can, I will forgive those I feel have wronged me. I will accept that I have been wronged, but I will not wrong myself by holding a grudge.

Persistence

"*We are made to persist. That's how we find out who we are.*"

❧TOBIAS WOLFF❧

There may be times when we feel like giving up. Everyone has these moments. Life is an adventure, and sometimes it's an adventure that gets the better of us.

But we keep on, and we will keep on. Around the next corner is something we haven't seen before. It could be something wonderful.

I will continue on this adventure of life as long as I can.